Sunset **Ideas for**

Hot Tubs, Spas & Home Saunas

By the Editors of Sunset Books
and Sunset Magazine

Lane Publishing Co., Menlo Park, California

Staff Editors:
Jack McDowell
Barbara G. Gibson
Julie Anne Gold

Design
Joe di Chiarro

Illustrations
Rik Olson, Terrence Meagher

Photography
All photos by Jack McDowell, except
as follows: Ed Bigelow—35, 37 top,
45 top, 48 top; Glenn Christiansen—
33 top; Ells Marugg—44, 51 top,
54 bottom left; John McCarthy—61
top; Jim Peck—49 bottom, 51 bottom;
Norm Plate—55 top, 60 top.

Cover
Home health center, featuring fiberglass spa and sauna, is also shown on
page 54, lower left. Photographed
by Clyde Childress.

Editor, Sunset Books
David E. Clark

Sixth printing February 1984

Acknowledgments

We'd like to extend our thanks to the
many organizations that helped bring
this book together: Aquarian Hot Tubs;
Barrel Builders; The Board and Barrel;
California Redwood Spa; The Colorado
Hot Tub Co.; Compool Corporation;
Creative Energy; Finnish-American
Sauna; Finska Sauna Corporation;
Galper and Baldon Landscape Archi-
tects; Hedon Hot Tubs; JBS Architec-
tural Specialties; Malibu Spa and
Pool; Metos Sauna of Portland; Neptune
Pools; Olympic Hot Tub Co.; Omi-
Lang Associates; Patricia Moore, Inc.;
Plantiques, Ltd.; Pool Water Products;
Rancho Soledad Nurseries, Inc.; The
Rocky Mountain Hot Tub Co.; San Juan
Pools of Denver; Sauna and Spa
Distributing Co.; Say Fromage; Snow-
mass Chamber of Commerce; Spa
Arama; Spa and Sauna Journal; Spa
World; Spring Mountain Hot Tubs; The
Tubmakers; Veldkamp's Flowers; Vico
Products Manufacturing Co.; Viking
Sauna of Northern California; Williams-
Sonoma of Beverly Hills; Wood in
the Round.

Special thanks go to the owners of the
installations appearing in the book, and
to the following individuals: Mikkel
Aaland; Cleo Baldon; Charles Barbara;
Ted Bassett; Dan Bello; Bernard T. Berba;
Buff Bradley; James Bukey; Carl Calvert;
Dan Christopherson; Chuck Fields;
Stan Freeman; Sid Galper; Veikko O.
Huttunen; William Kapranos; John T.
Kolkka; Peter Lieg; Rory Manley; Vi
Mathis; John A. Mensik; Gerald Moreland;
Chris Payne; Dr. Robert Stern; Edward
Stiles; Marilyn and Reino Tarkiainen;
Edward Turner; Jack Wyard.

Contents

Getting Yourself Into Hot Water

- **Hot tub or home spa?**
- **Basic planning**
- **Support equipment**
- **Installing the hot bath**
- **Shopping around**
- **Water treatment**
- **Maintenance**

Practiced as a form of physical therapy by many European cultures, refined as a mind-cleansing ritual by some Orientals, the hot soak has become a latter-day phenomenon in the United States. Most Americans use the hot soak to soothe tense muscles; others use it to relax the mind. But most everyone uses it because submerging the body in hot water feels good.

In this hot tub and spa primer you'll find a wealth of practical information on the vessels that hold the hot water—information that will help you make an intelligent decision as to which kind of hot tub or spa best suits your needs and desires, and how to put it where you want it.

Old wood cut *proves that tubs are not a new idea at all.*

To a rapidly growing number of Americans, hot tubs and spas conjure images of fun, frolic and friends in swirling hot waters. Still, a considerable number of people think a hot tub is what farm hands get into on Saturday night.

To clear up any misunderstandings, hot tubs and spas have little to do with the conventional American bath. Rather, they are watertight receptacles of all shapes, sizes and materials—wood, fiberglass, cement and metal—designed to hold 100° water and anywhere from one to a dozen bathers. An individual support equipment assembly (typically a heater, filter, and pump plus plumbing) keeps the water clean and stirs up a delightful, bubbling bath that people nationwide are discovering and jumping into with joy.

It's Ancient History

Though many ancient cultures—Roman, Egyptian, Greek, Turkish, and Japanese—enjoyed some form of communal hot bathing, the modern hot tub and spa can be most easily traced to its Roman and Japanese predecessors.

Ancient Roman baths had little to do with personal hygiene, a lot to do with good clean fun. Large and often boisterous aquatic arenas, these baths could accommodate thousands of people at one time. Here, one went to soak in the hot waters, relax, and socialize with friends.

For centuries the Japanese have enjoyed the pleasure of hot bathing in freestanding wooden tubs called *ofuros*. Unlike the large Roman forums, hot bathing in Japan was and is a family affair.

Though Americans are better known for their quick morning showers, hot water bathing has never been far from the American scene. Following the traditions of the great European resort spas, American resorts like Saratoga Springs, Warm Springs, and Calistoga quickly attracted rich patrons to their hot mineral waters.

Yankee Ingenuity

It was left to a group of fun-loving Californians to mix the conviviality of the Roman bath, the tranquility of the Japanese *ofuro,* and the therapeutic quality of hot mineral springs to come up with the prototype of the modern hot tub and spa.

At the turn of the century, Santa Barbara was a haven for the social elite seeking the pleasure of soaking in the nearby canyon hot springs. In the late 1960s, though the springs had long since lost their resort status, a group of bohemian Santa Barbarans decided to bring the joys of hot bathing from the canyons into their own back yards.

As if to dispel the myth that hot water bathing was a sport of the rich, they built their hot baths close to their homes, and from readily available materials. Scouring the countryside's farms and salvage yards, they collected a melange of wine vats, water

tanks, sidearm heaters, pipes, and pumps, and concocted some primitive but dearly loved hot tub systems. Word quickly spread of the new hedonistic pastime, and soon hot tub and spa companies proliferated.

Tubs and Spas Today

Whether in an indoor environment or out under the sky, hot tubs and spas soon become a way of life. Tub and spa owners find they soak anywhere from a few times a week to once or twice a day.

Just how warm the water should be is a continual point of contention. Though some hardy bathers boast of long endurance records at high temperatures, most health authorities recommend a maximum bathing temperature of 100°F for adults and 95° F for children.

If you've never experienced a hot bath the key is moderation. If you feel overcome by the heat, cool off for a few minutes outside the water. If you have a heart condition, circulatory problems or diabetes, or if you're pregnant, seek a doctor's advice before hot bathing.

Like their predecessors, modern tubs and spas are not cleansing vessels, so wash and rinse off before entering the water.

Tubs and spas cost less than in-ground swimming pools, often fit into small, previously unused space, and are relatively straightforward to install. Since they are smaller than swimming pools, they use less water, cost less to heat, and are easier to maintain. Not least, they're great fun to have around.

Most potential buyers know they want to buy a tub or spa, but that's about all they know. They are justifiably hesitant about pouring $3,000 or more into a young industry with few standards and even fewer controls.

To ease these concerns, let this book guide you through the major decisions involved in buying and installing a hot tub or spa—from design and planning to regular maintenance. In this way we hope to help you make intelligent choices so you can enjoy your new hot tub or spa to the fullest.

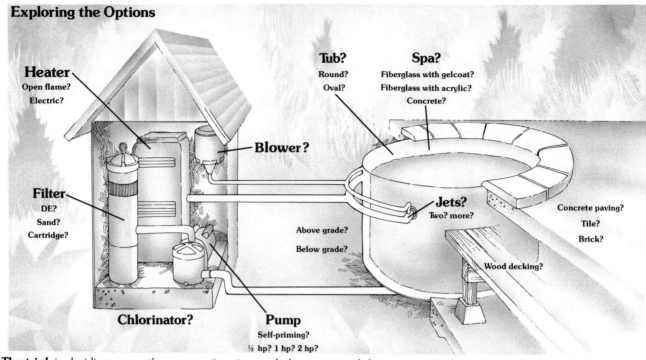

The **Heater**
Open flame?
Electric?

Tub?
Round?
Oval?

Spa?
Fiberglass with gelcoat?
Fiberglass with acrylic?
Concrete?

Blower?

Filter
DE?
Sand?
Cartridge?

Jets?
Two? more?

Concrete paving?
Tile?
Brick?

Above grade?

Below grade?

Wood decking?

Chlorinator?

Pump
Self-priming?
½ hp? 1 hp? 2 hp?

The trick in deciding among the many options is an orderly sequence of choice.

The Basic Choice— Spa or Tub?

The long, easy soak at the end of a long, hard day is a beautiful picture to develop in the mind's eye.

Getting from a dream to the reality of a hot tub or spa involves a long series of choices. Many are pleasant, some only gritty. All are necessary.

Although therapeutic heat and swirling waters are the same in either, choice No. 1 is between hot tub and spa.

A hot tub is usually round, straight-sided and of unstained redwood. But tubs can be oval or rectangular, have slanting sides, and be of cypress, oak, or other woods.

A spa usually is molded fiberglass with an inner lining of a hard, polished material. Forms and colors are as free as imagination cares to make them in these, and in less common spas of concrete or metal.

For most, the choice between these opposites is almost automatic because one or the other fits the family better: Soft, rustic tub or polished, sculpted spa.

However, the easy aesthetic choice is not always free to stand alone. There is the practical matter of money. Landscaping already in place may impose limitations. Finally come such long-range questions as portability, maintenance hours, and utility bills.

This section is a walk-through of the major elements of choice, starting with functional differences between tubs and spas. To keep you from making up your mind too soon, it should be noted there are vinyl liners for tubs and wooden casings for some spas.

Consider the Tub

Some tubs are recycled from original duty as wine tanks. Most new tubs are made just as wine tanks are, often by the same coopering firms.

Round or oval tub sides are beveled staves held in place by a dado joint at the floor and by metal hoops. Their floors rest on heavy joists, which in turn rest on concrete piers or solid pads. Constant soaking keeps tubs watertight without the use of a single nail.

Typically, tubs are 4 feet deep. They range from 2½ to 5 feet in depth. The most popular diameters are 5 and 6 feet, although they range down to 3½, up to 12 feet. (On rare occasion they exceed 12.) The standard 4 x 5 tub holds about 500 gallons of water, the 4 x 6 about 700. Full of water and bathers, such tubs weigh 7,000 to 8,000 pounds.

Wood. Vertical-grain all-heart redwood is the most-favored material for tubs. Properly maintained, it will last 15 years.

Other trees with similarly durable and usable heartwoods include cedar, cypress, and oak. Teak is a well-proven, though expensive wood.

The precise points of difference among the suitable woods do little to simplify choices.

Redwood is extremely resistant to decay, does not splinter, and swells easily to watertightness. It is not extremely resistant to damage from caustic chemicals.

Cedar comes very close to redwood on all counts; it is slightly less

The Basic Hot Tub

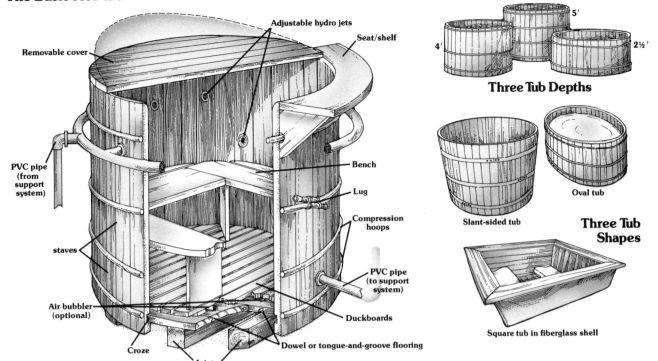

Labels (left tub cutaway):
- Removable cover
- Adjustable hydro jets
- Seat/shelf
- PVC pipe (from support system)
- Bench
- Lug
- Compression hoops
- staves
- PVC pipe (to support system)
- Air bubbler (optional)
- Duckboards
- Croze
- Dowel or tongue-and-groove flooring
- Joists

Three Tub Depths — 4′, 5′, 2½′

Three Tub Shapes — Slant-sided tub, Oval tub, Square tub in fiberglass shell

Tubs offer a surprising range of choices in size and shape, as well as equipment.

resistant to decay, slightly more resistant to chemical damage. It may not be as long-lived.

Oak, a hardwood, has as its principal weakness a tendency to decay. Well-maintained, it is extremely durable.

Teak is the unchallenged champion in durability and decay resistance. Also, it has a natural oily smoothness. Price and availability are the drawbacks.

All wood types should be kiln- as opposed to air-dried. Kiln-dried wood absorbs moisture more evenly, so is less likely to twist or buckle in use, and thus is less likely to develop leaks.

At publication, average-sized redwood tubs ran between $800 and $1,200. Cedar tubs cost as much as $200 less. Oak was priced almost two times more than redwood in some markets. Teak is the most expensive wood of them all.

There are regional variations. For example, oak is closer in price to redwood near the oak forests of Kentucky than it is next to the redwoods in California.

It is possible to cut costs on a tub by choosing lesser cuts than heartwood. The risks are water leaks through weak spots and splintering.

The price of a tub is only one leg of a triangle.

Add pump, filter, heater and the rest of a support system to the price of a redwood tub, and a typical unit costs in the range of $2,000 to $3,000 before installing.

The price range may seem extraordinary, especially since it can be more than double the cost of the tub itself. Still, only a small part of the variation owes itself to regional differences. Far the greater part stems from the wide array of choices in mechanical supports to the tub or spa. Pumps alone range more than $100 apart in price, and the new tub or spa buyer has not only that choice, but the option of using two, and an air blower to boot. The other elements are almost as variable.

At publication, professionals charged between $1,000 and $1,500 for an above-grade installation on a reasonably accessible site. (Because tubs are self-supporting by their nature, they lend themselves to above-grade locations.)

Since above-grade site work is relatively simple, this is an area in which most homeowners save money at the expense of personal labor. Skilled handymen often can do some or all of the plumbing and electrical work as well.

Once a tub is installed, maintenance is somewhat more time-consuming than a spa's because wood is soft-textured, and because staves and seats make nooks and crannies. Wood also may deteriorate more sharply than the hard surface of a spa when maintenance is poor.

Tubs have a distinct edge over spas in portability. Above-grade installation makes them possible to pick up and carry away. The loss is in abandoning part or all of the foundation and in sawn up PVC connections.

Spas rarely lend themselves to such uprooting because they are dug into the good earth.

Fiberglass and Concrete Spas

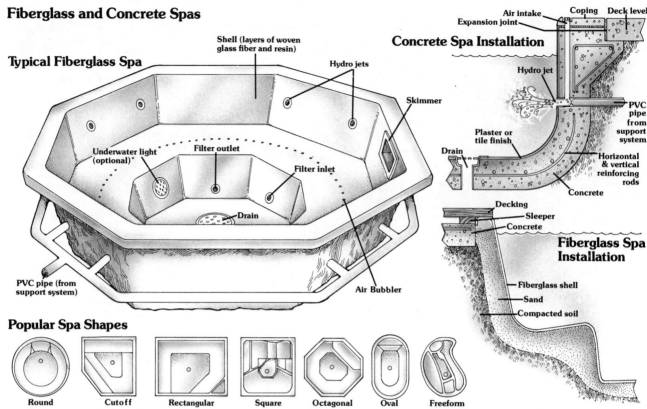

Typical Fiberglass Spa

Shell (layers of woven glass fiber and resin)

Hydro jets

Skimmer

Underwater light (optional)

Filter outlet

Filter inlet

Drain

PVC pipe (from support system)

Air Bubbler

Concrete Spa Installation

Air intake — Coping — Deck level

Expansion joint

Hydro jet

Plaster or tile finish

Drain

PVC pipe from support system

Horizontal & vertical reinforcing rods

Concrete

Decking

Sleeper

Concrete

Fiberglass Spa Installation

Fiberglass shell

Sand

Compacted soil

Popular Spa Shapes

Round   Cutoff   Rectangular   Square   Octagonal   Oval   Freeform

Freedom of form characterizes spas, which are best-suited to below-grade installation.

Regard the Spa

Originally the gunite spa was about the only residential type sold, and then as an adjunct to swimming pools. Once hot tubs appeared, though, fiberglass shells were quick to follow in every size, shape and color imaginable.

Although their shapes are far more variable, spas still tend to follow the basic size of hot tubs—typical ones are close to 4 feet deep, and 5 to 6 feet across, but they can be found somewhat smaller and much larger.

After shape, the two qualities that set spas apart from tubs are the facts that they come as a single piece, and have hard inner surfaces.

Fiberglass shells. A great majority of spas are molded fiberglass shells with either an acrylic or gelcoat inner lining. These shells are supported,

bottom and sides, by sand. This requires below-grade installation, or some sort of retaining wall for above-grade placement.

Quality in fiberglass spas is somewhat more difficult to assess than in tubs. Vertical-grain heartwood looks like what it is: knot-free wood with the grain running true from one end of the piece to the other. The surest test of quality in fiberglass is the manufacturer's reputation. (The design or shape is not a test. Well known molds are subject to copy by competitors less quality conscious than the originator.) Points to check on the spot are: Consistent thickness along the edges (the only places where line-of-sight will work), and absence of cracks or creases anywhere. Well made molds will show reinforcing at the steps, across the bottom, and around all outlets. The interior lining should be blemish-free. One other sign of quality is smoothness in the tile work set at water level in some spas. (Ostensibly the tile is there to ease maintenance. In fact the

grouting is harder to keep clean than either gelcoat or acrylic. The idea is a hangover from concrete spas, in which tile is easier to clean than the relatively rough plaster finish.)

The relative merits of acrylic versus gelcoat linings are a subject of some debate. It is not easy to regard one or the other as a superior choice. Acrylic, a harder material, is more resistant to abrasion damage than is gelcoat. It also withstands chemical damage and high temperatures more readily.

Gelcoat performs well in all these departments, and is less expensive. Gelcoat also is a good deal easier and less expensive to repair if time or accident should damage the finish.

Whichever lining, fiberglass spas tend to be slightly more expensive than wooden tubs of comparable quality.

In addition, installation costs usually run higher for fiberglass spas than for tubs. Although a few designs are self-supporting, most must be buttressed all around. This means either digging a hole or building up a masonry support, then backfilling with sand once the shell is in place and connected to its plumbing system. Typically, contractors priced such installation between $1,500 and $2,000 at publication time.

Maintenance of spas is quicker and easier than for tubs. The smooth, comparatively non-porous surfaces wipe clean more easily than wood can be scrubbed. Many come with built-in skimmers to help keep solids out of the bath water.

Concrete spas. Concrete spas started as adjuncts to swimming pools. That still is how most come into being.

Concrete's principal advantage is great durability coupled with easy maintenance of a hard cement finish. Specifically, maintenance of a plaster or other cement finish falls midway in difficulty and time required between wood tubs and the harder, smoother acrylic and gelcoat surfaces. (Concrete spas should have a tile ring at water level since algae tend to form and cling there, and tile is easier to wipe clean than is plaster.)

Four methods can be used to build a concrete spa; masonry block, hand-packed concrete, poured concrete, and gunite.

Gunite, though requiring special-ized equipment, is the most common method now used. (See page 24 for a fuller explanation of the process.)

It can become reasonably eco-nomical as a companion piece to a gunite swimming pool if both are installed at the same time and both use the same support system.

Metal spas. Sculpted as fiberglass or gunite may be, there are vast realms beyond for those with long supplies of money and access to metal sculptors, who can fashion whimsical pigs, or copies of claw-foot bathtubs, or any other fancy. Because these are such personal projects, nothing can be said here except that the opportunities are legion.

An exception to this generality about metal spas is an aluminum one lined with chlorinated rubber. These, however, remain new enough and rare enough that little is known about durability or other factors of choice.

Operating Costs

Hot tubs and spas require pumps, filters and heaters—as described in detail on pages 18-19. The on-going costs for utilities to operate these are significant, with the main bill being for heat.

Most heaters are fired with natural gas or propane. A broad survey showed that gas-fired hot tubs and spas added between $15 and $25 to monthly utility bills at publication. Electric heaters cost two to three times more in most areas. However, these figures must be taken only as the roughest of guides. Rates are climbing steadily. Also, frequency of use is so variable as to defy a fair guess on any individual bill.

Electricity for pumps and lights (if any) will add at least a few dollars a month to utility bills.

A separate cost is chemicals to keep water in good condition. A typical monthly bill is $5 to $15 (see pages 28-30.)

Taxes and Credits

Before leaving money considerations behind, it may be useful to note how hot tubs and spas affect property taxes, and how they may be used to gain tax credits under some circumstances.

As permanent structures, tubs and spas will be considered real property and assessed at full market value of the installation. This value then will be added to the real property value of your home, and taxed accordingly.

The most typical deduction is medical.

To qualify for a medical deduction, a tub or spa must be used to treat a specific illness or condition. A physician's prescription for general health purposes will not be allowed.

Anyone seeking to claim a medical deduction should get knowledgeable tax advice before making a purchase. Also required: a competent appraisal of the property before and after installation of tub or spa.

The cost, or capital expense, in this case can only be deducted to the extent it exceeds the value the improvement adds to a property. So, for example, if a tub installation costs $4,000, but adds only $3,000 to the property value, the capital deduction can only be $1,000.

Another tax credit is possible if you sell your property. A seller can deduct the cost of a tub or spa (and other real improvements) from his profit on the sale, thereby reducing his capital gains.

First Caveat

In buying a tub or spa, shop around for everything . . . equipment, supplier, contractor, designer.

This is the only way to get an accurate picture of what is available and what it should cost.

Last Caveat

Get proper building permits from city or county for all work before beginning construction. Do-it-yourselfers must get their own. Homeowners who have hired contractors should see permits posted on the site before allowing work to begin.

There are fees for permits—flat in some communities, proportional to price in others—but this cost is nothing compared to the problems permits solve if or when something goes wrong with the work. Without a permit, there is the risk of having to tear out completed work at your expense. Worse, lack of permits may be a ground for a supplier or manu-facturer to invalidate warranties or guarantees under an improper use clause.

The Opportunities in Landscaping

However much pleasure a tub or spa brings while it is being used, it remains a sizeable part of the landscape during all the other hours of the day.

It needs to look like more than a utility vessel or a puddle.

How to achieve a handsome setting raises a host of questions. For many, a basic requirement is comfortable sitting or sprawling space right next to the tub. Decks and patios become both a requirement and an opportunity to build eye-catching changes of level into the tub environment.

In some climates, what goes overhead is even more important to comfort than what is underfoot. Sheltering devices can make even bolder statements than decks.

Still, more important than any visual fine point is the need to locate the tub or spa where it can be used most comfortably.

One of the time-honored distinctions between going for a swim and having a bath is that you do not have to wear a suit for the latter. If this is a factor, the tub or spa might fit your plans better if it is close to the house—or even indoors—rather

than clear at the back corner of the property. This may be especially true if all of the neighbors have taller houses than your fence can hide.

In the next seven pages we try to raise all of the major landscaping questions to help you assess your individual opportunities.

As a first step, check into local zoning requirements concerning setbacks, height limitations, and related legal limits. (One other, most important legal consideration is that tubs and spas should have secure covers to keep children out of the water when they are not supervised. Courts have held that pools, spas and similar bodies of water are attractive nuisances, and that fencing alone is not a legally adequate barrier to a child. Some tub and spa covers have locks to meet this express situation.)

Dealing with Grade Levels

As the sketches below indicate, the flat lot owner will have an easy time putting a wooden tub above ground, or a spa shell below grade. But being contrary will cost money and pose special technical or construction problems.

Putting a tub in a below-grade pit involves work well beyond the average homeowner's ability. In essence, one must make a sump to

hold the tub, then another, deeper sump to drain the first one. The finished concrete shell must also be large enough to guarantee free air circulation around the tub, since a constant humid atmosphere will lead to decay in the wood.

The tub's pump-filter-heater assembly must remain at grade to avoid risk of short circuits in case of flooding in the pit.

Putting a spa above grade is not so difficult as putting a tub below ground level although the process can be expensive.

The basic requirement—and the major expense—is a surrounding wall of whatever height the designer wishes. (Typically, the change in level should make a comfortable seat.) Masonry materials are the most logical candidates for such walls.

How far the wall is to be from the spa's edge has much to do with final cost since the area inside almost certainly will be filled with sand. (Proper support of a spa requires nine inches of sand all around. However, the sand must be surrounded in turn by solid material; loose earth cannot be used, so a built-up area wider than the minimum also requires sand fill.)

People faced with a sloping site can—in practical terms—choose between an above-grade tub or below-grade spa with almost equal ease, but not quite. As the sketches

Dealing with Grades

Naturally Easy

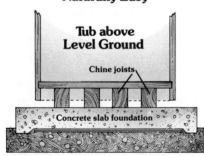

Middle Ground

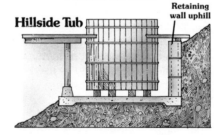

Fighting Nature

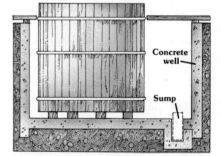

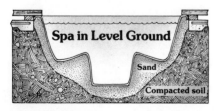

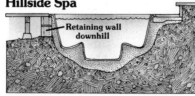

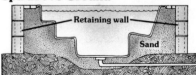

show, the tub may require a full-fledged retaining wall while the spa may need a lesser and less critical sort of wall.

Where Will a Tub/Spa Work Best for You?

Budget yourself a block of time to find the right setting for your tub or spa. There are advantages to both indoor and outdoor locations—you should choose the one that suits your needs and budget, as well as your climate and landscape.

When picking an out-of-doors spot for your tub or spa (for indoor spas see page 16), make a scale drawing of your property like the one shown above right. On a sheet of graph paper show:
• Lot dimensions.
• Location of house on lot (including doors and windows and the rooms from which they open).
• Points of the compass—north, south, east, and west.
• Path of the sun and any hot spots it produces.
• Utilities (water, gas, and sewers) and underground wires that could affect your hot tub/spa location. (Units never should be located beneath utility wires.)
• Setback boundaries (your city or county building department can tell you what they are).
• Direction of prevailing winds.
• Existing garden structures.
• Existing plants and trees.
• Problems beyond the lot line which may affect sun, view, or privacy, such as unsightly telephone wires, major plantings, or a neighbor's second-story window.

If you live on a sloping lot, it's also a good idea to draw a second map showing the lot's contours, high and low spots, and natural drainage patterns.

With your "base map" drawn, cover it with tracing paper and try out your ideas. As you sketch, think about ease of tub/spa installation, the visual effect in the garden or indoors, and climate and terrain factors that will influence an outdoor site. Consider, too, the traffic patterns likely to be followed by tubbers.

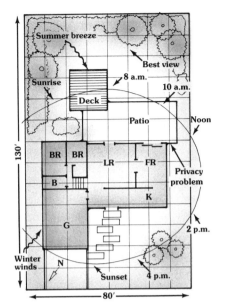

Getting a plan on paper is your first step in choosing an outdoor location for your hot tub or spa. Using graph paper, make a scale drawing of your property; show lot dimensions, house location, plants, trees, and garden structures, and any weather or privacy problems that might interfere with your hot bath enjoyment.

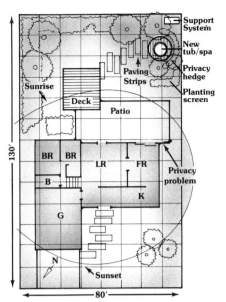

Sample plan, sketched on tracing paper placed over the scale drawing, shows one way a tub or spa might fit into an existing landscape. Located in a seldom-used corner of the lot, the spa becomes an eye-catching focal point. Screened with trees and a hedge, it is protected from wind, afternoon sun, and neighbors' lines of vision.

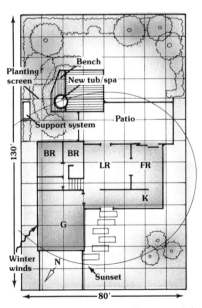

Alternate plan connects the new tub/spa to an existing low-level deck. Here, in an intermediate zone of the yard, the tub is near enough the house to be easily accessible, far enough away to remain a significant visual element in the garden. With a wood lid and benches, the spa unit doubles as an outdoor entertaining area.

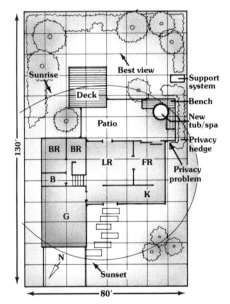

Tub/spa located nearest the house has the advantage of a sunny southern exposure, less costly installation (shorter plumbing and wiring distances), and easy access during wintry days when the tub or spa is most likely to be used. Nearness to household noise, however, can lessen tubbing's relaxing benefits.

Making the Most of the Odd-shaped Lot

One of the secrets of landscaping—whether you're incorporating a tub or spa into an existing garden, or planning a garden from scratch—is knowing how to turn liabilities into assets. Awkwardly shaped lots, small garden spaces, and steeply-sloping sites all depend on design imagination to make them both functional and visually appealing.

For the square-shaped lot shown at right, for instance, a circular approach relieves the strong angular lines of house and lot. To give the yard a lengthier look, focal points lie at each end: a hot tub is tucked into a circle of trees at one, a garden greenhouse at the other.

Primary drawbacks to the wedge-shaped lot below were its sharply-angled corners and unequally divided outdoor spaces. Solution to the sharp corners was plantings to camouflage and soften them; solution to the irregular outdoor spaces was to make one of them open and expansive, the other more private and sheltered . . . a perfect setting for tub or spa.

Study these approaches to making the best use of space in four typically odd-shaped lots: they illustrate how effective design can minimize eccentric features in a landscape. (Arrows on the drawings indicate the direction a viewer's attention is drawn by the landscape elements.)

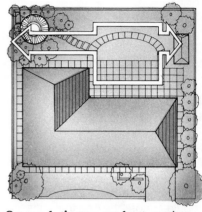

Square lot's rear garden *is made to seem less square with arc in lawn, and longer with focal points at each end. Leaving the house one may look left toward the hot tub, which is sheltered in a circle of trees (and accessible from the main patio or master bedroom), or right toward a garden greenhouse.*

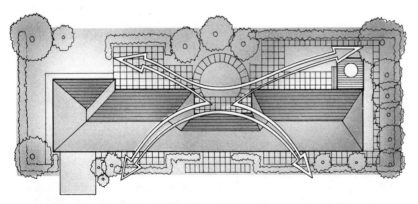

In a wedge-shaped lot, *irregular outdoor spaces lend themselves nicely to distinct activity zones. A generous open lawn area in one corner provides plenty of play space; a small patio area in another provides a more private climate for tubbing. Plantings soften the lot's sharp corners.*

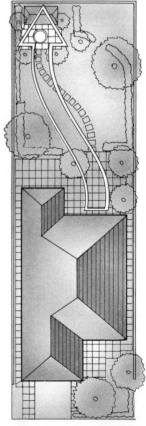

Long, narrow lot *has a barber-pole look to it unless its space can be divided into at least two distinct, offset areas. Here, an S-curved axis leads the eye across one garden to an open-air spa and spa-side shelter. A modest grade in this type lot can also add to visual interest with different horizontal levels.*

You can give an extremely shallow lot *a feeling of greater depth if you are able to create focal points at the lot line with built-in benches, garden walks, or eye-catching plantings. Where setback limitations thwart you, break up the yard's length with a series of outdoor living areas. Here there are four, with the spa at one end.*

Consider Your Climate

Evaluate climate conditions peculiar to your property before you install a tub or spa outdoors. Understanding seasonal sun and wind patterns that affect your lot will help you choose a setting that maximizes your hot bath enjoyment.

The seasonal sun. You've probably noticed that the sun generates varying amounts of shade on your property according to its seasonal position in the sky (see illustrations below). In the winter, shadows on the north side of the house are deeper, in the summer much shorter.

The Sun by Seasons

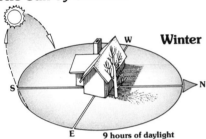

Winter

9 hours of daylight

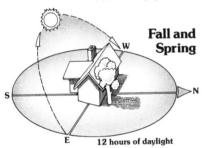

Fall and Spring

12 hours of daylight

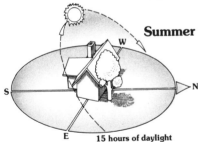

Summer

15 hours of daylight

As a general rule, a tub or spa situated on the north side of the house will almost always be in shade —an advantage if you live in a hot desert climate and want to protect your spa from the sun's hot midsummer rays.

If yours is a cool climate, the best setting for your tub may be on the south side of the house where it can take advantage of full sun. A tub on the east side receives morning sun, and a tub on the west, sun in the afternoon.

Dealing with wind. Next, study wind patterns around your house and lot. Too much wind blowing over your tub or spa on a cool day can be as unpleasant as no wind at all on a hot summer day. Excess wind around a spa also can kick up enough dust to tax its filter and pump, encourage evaporation and cool the water temperature.

To pinpoint wind currents in your yard, try posting small flags where you want wind protection and observe their movements during windy periods. Observe, too, in the following illustrations the effects different barriers have on wind to learn which type of fence or screen best suits your needs.

Screening against Wind

Unchecked exposure to wind rapidly cools the water in a tub or spa, kicks up dust, and puts an unnecessary strain on the support system. Fences or screens of plants can modify breezes.

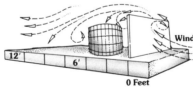

Wind washes over a solid fence as a stream of water would wash over a solid barrier. About the distance equal to fence height, protection drops rapidly.

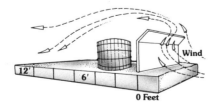

Angling baffle into the wind gives greatest protection close to the fence, but effective protection also extends to a distance more than twice fence height.

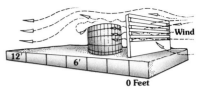

To break wind flow, choose fence with laths spaced 1/2 inch apart, or screens of plants. Up close, the fence offers relatively little protection; temperatures are warmest at a distance equal to about twice fence height. Shrubbery, if dense, would yield more shelter.

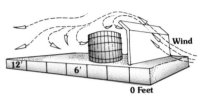

A 45° baffle at top of fence eliminates the downward crash of wind. You feel warmest in the pocket below the baffle and about 6 feet from the 6-foot-high fence. Beyond that point, temperature change is minimal.

Dealing with winter. Tubs and spas can be kept usable through winters at the expense of extra hours of heater use. When the weather does not lend itself to outdoor soaking, thermostats on tank heaters can be lowered to temperatures too cool for baths, but warm enough to safeguard tub or spa and support system plumbing from freezing. Special "hydro-stat" sensors can be used with coil heaters for the same purpose.

During severe freezes, all support systems should be drained even if insulated and/or sheltered. Spas also should be drained, but tubs cannot be allowed to dry. (One manufacturer says a tub should never be left without water more than two days.) Tubs must be plumbed to allow draining the support system without draining the tub.

One other cautionary note: In snow country, do not place tubs or spas beneath eavelines. Falling snow can crush them.

How to Frame Your Tub or Spa

Except on the rarest of occasions, your hot tub or spa needs a setting like a painting needs a frame. If your garden happens to be a grove of redwood trees, of course a tub standing alone among them can be visual dynamite. But if you're planning to install a spa into your standard-lot garden, you need to think about an appropriate frame, wood or masonry, that will integrate it into the landscape in a pleasing way. A hot tub plugged into a bare patch of lawn offers little in the way of visual interest.

To decide whether you want your hot tub/spa to serve as a major focal point or as a more subtle element in the landscape, consider how it will affect the overall appearance of the yard. Will it complement or compete with other features—a handsome patio or deck, gazebo, or swimming pool? Will an above-grade tub overwhelm nearby low-growing plants you prize? Or will it balance garden plantings? Will it blend or will it clash with the architectural style of your house?

If you choose to make your tub or spa a garden focal point, consider raising it above grade and framing it with built-in benches. If you want a more subtle effect, install your tub/spa flush with decking or paving. If you install it above ground, it can still be made to seem unobtrusive if you soften its features with plants.

Raised decking, *built-in benches, and existing evergreens provide a balanced setting for above-grade tub, situated in a seldom-used corner of the lot.*

Hillside deck *proves a handsome match of fiberglass and wood. Design: Chaffee-Zumwalt Assoc.*

Concrete spa *is separated from the swimming pool with a broad tile seat. Design: Don Brandeau.*

Radiating redwood planks *and ring of star jasmine make a simple, bold frame for a ground-level tub.*

Installed flush *with a new deck, tub sits half above an existing brick patio, half below. Design: Don Brandeau.*

Gaining a Sense of Shelter

If your tub/spa is outdoors and you live in a temperate climate, there's usually no need to provide overhead protection. Periodic hot soaks right in the rain are, for many tubbers, wonderfully refreshing. If, though, you live in an area such as the Northwest, where rain is a dependable constant during long winter months —or if the sun beats a hot path to your spa in the summer—you may wish to cover yourself with a more substantial roof.

The illustrations below suggest your broad range in options. With the sky as their cover, owners of the open-air tub (bottom left) have the advantage of stargazing at night and skygazing in the afternoon. Only a long stretch of hard rains keeps them from the pleasures of a good hot soak. Likewise, owners of a fiberglass spa (center) prefer an open-air setting, although they added a dressing room and sauna so rainy-day tubbers and sauna bathers would have a sheltered spot to cool down.

Between no roof and a solid roof lies a compromise—lath or lattice structures that admit the sun but give a feeling of protection—such as the lath roof at bottom right. You also can often buy prefabricated lath structures for tubs and spas from local dealers.

For solid protection you can go as far as a shingle-roofed gazebo that offers permanence as well as protection from sun and rain. Or you can shelter your spa with an airy greenhouse-style glass roof (top right) that keeps out the rain but lets in the light—a decided disadvantage if you live in a climate where the sun makes the spa area uncomfortably hot.

Solid-roofed gazebo *offers permanent shelter from sun and rain and makes a handsome garden focal point. Design: Lyman Seely.*

Adjoining sauna/dressing *room is handy when rainy-day bathers need a sheltered spot to cool down.*

Fine views *may make no roof the most desirable solution. If so, under-seat shelter for equipment can be useful. Design: Ed Hoiland.*

Tempered glass *in a wood frame gives rain protection without shutting out the light or overhead view. Design: Brad Brown.*

Lath roof *gives partial shade and a sense of shelter for hillside spa. Design: Donald G. Boos.*

Screening Your Spa for Weather and Privacy

Vertical screens—made from wood, canvas, glass, bamboo, and plants—can make a big contribution where you need privacy or wind protection. Depending on their design and location (and your climate—see page 13), vertical screens will modify wind, block sun, muffle noise from too-near neighbors, and—in the case of spas and tubs—separate them from more prominent areas of the garden.

With climate as your guide, determine which type of screen best suits your needs. A solid wood screen like the one shown below, for example, offers maximum privacy but minimum wind protection for the close-by tub.

If you need privacy for a spa in a shaded corner of the garden, consider using translucent white fiberglass in a wood frame. It can screen out a neighbor's line of sight without cutting out the light.

Where you wish to block wind without losing a view, consider using clear plastic or tempered glass panels.

Many of the most appealing screens are created with plants and trees. They give a soft, natural feeling to a tub or spa setting while they work to help disperse brisk winds, protect from hot sun, cushion noise, and cool the climate around them. You can screen with evergreen shrubs, vines on wood trellises—almost anything—although you should choose plants according to their growth rate, ultimate size, texture, color, shape, and habit. Avoid those that attract bees or shed debris over the area.

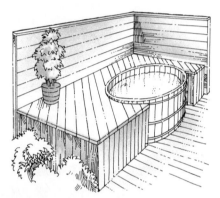

Solid wood fence *frames oval tub and provides privacy by screening out a neighbor's view*

Walls of wood-framed glass *surround view-oriented tub to give tubbers and plants wind protection. Doors slide open and shut on tracks.*

Lattice screen, *designed to separate tub area from the rest of the garden, is softened with colorful vine. Design: Donald G. Boos.*

Louvered fence *modifies wind and block's neighbor's line of sight without cutting off the view*

The Indoor Look of Tubs & Spas

A number of tub and spa enthusiasts prefer an indoor setting for their spa, for several reasons.

There's the obvious advantage of having the tub or spa sheltered and accessible day and night, year round. (In harsh climates it's often necessary to have an indoor site that allows complete control over the environment—not only of the water, but the support system plumbing as well.)

Where privacy is essential, but impossible to achieve in the garden, the house will provide it.

Where the safety of children—especially neighboring children—is difficult to assure at an outdoor site, lockable doors solve all manner of legal and personal worries.

Compelling as one or more of these reasons may be, they do not make the difficult task of keeping a tub or spa inside any easier. Integrating a tub or spa into household routine takes a good deal of thought. As one side effect, these vessels are marvelously efficient manufacturers of humidity—a plus if you live in a dry climate where air moisture is a scarcity, an uncomfortable handicap if your air is characteristically heavy with humidity.

Deciding on an indoor location. As anyone who has had to fit a new bed into a well-ordered house knows, an object 5 feet across cannot be slipped into a place unnoticed. When it is for such a singular purpose as a tub or spa is, the task of fitting it into a working household becomes doubly difficult.

Shaping the Indoor Setting

Adjustable skylight — lets hot air escape

Exhaust vent

Sliding glass doors — help regulate air circulation

Rust-resistant fixtures

Opening windows — improve ventilation

Wood paneling — insulates and absorbs moisture

Moisture-loving plants

Wood or foam cover — prevents steaming, reduces heat loss from water

Support system (properly vented)

Fresh air vent

Wood decking — insulates and absorbs moisture, allows drainage

Concrete floor and foundation (sloped toward drain)

Drain (from tub to main sewage line)

Consider all the above elements when you plan an indoor tub or spa. Under normal use, tubs and spas create enormous clouds of vapors; if yours is indoors you need to build a room around it that can manage a marine climate. Other than wood, ceramic tiles often are used as an indoor spa flooring material.

Think first of traffic patterns. To be an oasis of calm, the tub or spa will have to be away from comings and goings of people in a hurry. This means putting it in a room that does not carry through traffic, or one that serves several other important purposes.

Try to locate your tub/spa near a dressing area; trails of water in areas well away from the tub can be a nuisance to clean up.

Try, too, to locate your indoor spa within reasonable reach of the outdoors. Even a nook-size deck or patio nearby can make a pleasant place to relax between soaks.

Questions about construction.

Once the problems of location are solved, the special requirements of construction must be faced. Weight and humidity are the two most complex and vital concerns.

Standard floors are designed and built to support 40 pounds per square foot. A small hot tub or spa, filled with water and one or two bathers can easily apply 250 pounds to the same square foot. For this reason, it's critically important to provide an adequate foundation. To support a tub safely, an existing wood frame floor (say in a spare bedroom) usually requires re-engineering; often even a concrete slab in the basement must be replaced with a thicker, reinforced slab.

The requirements your building code sets for an indoor tub's foundation, plumbing and wiring—coupled with the need for efficient ventilation —explain why the best time to think about an indoor spa is in new construction or as a room addition. Major remodeling within an existing building is unquestionably the most problematical route to a hot soak.

In addition to having an adequate substructure for the tub, flooring must be sloped toward a drain and made of materials—ceramic tile, sheet vinyl, concrete, flagstone, or masonry —that aren't affected by large doses of water. (Wood decking, constructed above a concrete slab or drain field, also is useful as a flooring surface

for indoor spas. It absorbs some moisture, allows excess to drain through, and provides a degree of noise insulation.)

Walls and ceilings must have insulation with a vapor barrier to resist moisture. (This applies to interior as well as exterior walls; the rest of the house must be protected against excess humidity from tub or spa.)

Controlling condensation.

Efficient ventilation is your best means of controlling condensation that can collect on walls, windows, and ceiling, even when the tub or spa is not in use.

To have maximum control over your indoor climate it may be necessary to back up natural cross ventilation with a forced air system.

In addition to ventilation, plan on double-glazed windows and skylights that inhibit condensation. Moisture-loving plants and walls paneled with unfinished wood are useful because they absorb excess moisture.

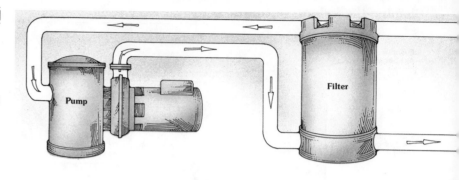

The Support System

The mechanical devices described on these pages and the one following are what distinguish tubs and spas from bathtubs, however unorthodox the latter might be.

As opposed to standard household plumbing, in these recirculating systems a filter keeps the water clean so it can be re-used instead of being drained away each time, a heater keeps the water hot for as long as you want to soak instead of letting it sag to lukewarm then cold, and a pump keeps the water moving for the above reasons and also to power jets, which make a soak therapeutic as well as relaxing.

On the other side of the coin, they mean that soap is not allowed in the tub because it gums up the machinery.

The choices between tubs and spas are based on major differences. The choices among all the possible pumps, filters, heaters and small pieces grow far more subtle. Not only are there many models of each element, but all the parts of the system have to fit together in harmony as well.

The capacity of the pump cannot be too much greater or less than those of filter and heater, or things will go awry all along the line.

On these pages is some basic information about the major elements's operating principles, sizes, and materials to help you consider which choices will function well in your situation.

On page 20 are some hints on how to integrate the separate elements into an efficient system . . . or how to assess the qualities of package deals.

Because systems are complex engineering jobs, many suppliers offer components of their choice. Some even pre-plumb these packages, mounting them on a pallet. All the buyer has to do is connect the assembly as required. While many packages are well designed, they should not be accepted blindly. Some of the budget models may be sadly underpowered for their job.

How Pumps Work

All pumps move water by sucking it in one side and pushing it out the other.

Centrifugal pumps produce high flow rates with low pressure. Most are 3/4 to 2 horsepower for spa use, which translates to 55 to 105 gallons per minute at level. (The gpm decreases with each foot the pump must raise water.)

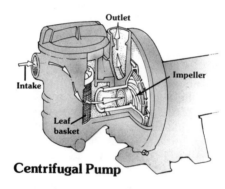

Centrifugal Pump

Although some can be wired for 115 volts, the recommendation is for 230 volts in nearly every case.

These pumps are made of bronze and brass and various plastics.

Bronze and brass are durable, usually lasting 5 to 10 years, sometimes going 20. (Their motors last three to four years on average.) To justify their high price they must be used steadily over a long time.

Plastic does not corrode, but not all types are durable. Those made of Noryl have a reputation for greater durability than others. Plastic must be guarded against freezing and over-heating.

At publication, prices of 1 hp pumps ranged from $220 to $275 for plastic, $250 to $350 for bronze.

Filter Functions

Filters remove solids from water by trapping them in material finer than they are. For pools and spas there are three choices: cartridge, DE (diatomaceous earth) and sand.

Cartridge. Rigid frames have fine liners of dacron, polyester, or a treated paper. The cartridges fit tightly into a flow chamber so all water must pass through them.

The system is the least expensive, and also provides the least fine filtration. Most cartridge systems accept two or more filters because a relatively large filtering surface is required to be effective; 50 square feet is typical.

Cartridges last 1 to 2 years, then must be replaced.

DE. Diatomaceous earth, a fine, chalky material, is forced against rigid permeable plates by water pressure. Solids then embed in the DE.

This is the most expensive filter type, and gives the tightest filtration with the smallest surface.

Sand. Sand yields a slightly less tight filtration than DE, but a finer one

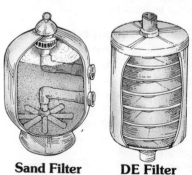

Sand Filter   **DE Filter**

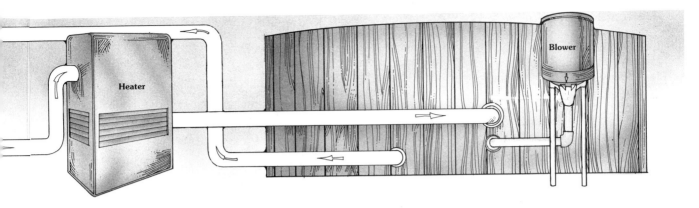

than cartridge filters. Units are about the same size as comparable D.E. types, but rated on a different scale.

Prices range from $140-200 for cartridge, $260-300 for D.E., and $240-310 for sand, all with 50 gpm capacity.

How Heaters Work

The economics of fuel make it the first concern of people choosing a heater for tub or spa.

The major choices are open-flame (natural gas, propane, heating oil) and electric.

Open-flame. Three sub-types are available—coil, tank and convection.

Coil heaters—also known as flash heaters—present a small, fast-moving volume of water to a large flame for fast heating. Such heaters are rated at 85,000 to 200,000 BTU (British Thermal Units) capacity.

Tank heaters present a large volume of slow-moving or still water to a relatively small flame, just as home water heaters do. Rated at 20,000 to 40,000 BTU, they are less expensive to buy than coil heaters. The drawbacks are long recovery periods, and inefficiency in cold climates when they must produce large increases in water temperature.

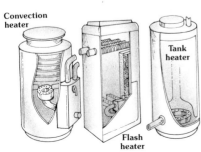

Convection heater

Tank heater

Flash heater

Convection heaters, with or without small, separate booster pump, are a hybrid of the other two, using a large coil to heat slow-moving water. Inexpensive to buy, and operate, they further allow (or demand) scaling back other support equipment. Many recommend against jets or bubblers with these heaters because they are slowest to heat water the last few degrees —the crucial few when water is highly active.

Electric heaters. Much like small gas-fired tank heaters in performance, most are rated at 20,000 to 40,000 BTU, equivalent. (The actual ratings are 6 to 12 Kw; some small units use 6 Kw heaters.) They are slow to heat, especially when large increases are required. The greater drawback in most areas is high cost of electricity.

Most are wired at 230 volts.

Electric heaters typically cost between $200 and $350. Gas-fired tank heaters run in the range of $500-700. Most coil types range from $400 to $450, but deluxe models top $600.

Covers. Tub and spa covers and insulation blankets should be thought of as extensions of the heater. Properly used, they reduce the load on a heater by half or more.

Wood covers for tubs cost between $170 and $250 for a 5-foot diameter. Fiberglass covers—more efficient and equally durable—range from $45 to $150. Pliable insulation blankets can be used alone or paired with a rigid cover. Depending on size, they cost between $25 and $55. Thermal covers—the most energy efficient—cost between $200 and $400.

Activating the Water

The basic mover of water in a tub or spa is the pump. To give a real sensation of moving water, the pump is boosted with venturi jets, a blower, or both.

A venturi jet, also called hydro jet in the trade, restricts the flow of water in a tube, thereby increasing its velocity.

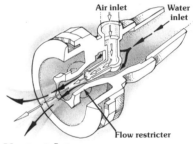

Venturi Jet

Venturis can be fixed units, or have a swivelling eyeball to allow changing direction of flow. Some have a separate air intake to produce bubbles.

Blowers produce more intense bubble action than a venturi alone by mixing air at the venturi, or through separate rings. They are separate from the main pump, usually controlled by their own switch so bubbles can be options.

Not incidentally, these air pumps must be at least 12 inches above water level, or must be protected by air loops and check valves.

Designing a System

Once the basic choice of tub or spa is made, and a site chosen, the next task is to work out details of the support system.

The general goal is to get a team of matched pacers—parts that work compatibly one with another.

The pump is the heart of any system. It must provide enough power to make all the other components work. Jets do much to govern pump size.

System 1 shows a standard 4 x 5 tub or spa with a typical support package. It uses a ¾ or 1 hp pump, has two jets, a cartridge filter with 50 gpm of filtering capacity, and a 145,000 BTU gas-fired coil heater. (The heater could be replaced with a smaller one.) Going toward more sophistication, the cartridge filter could be replaced with a DE type for finer filtering.

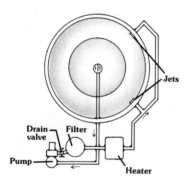

One manufacturer recommends a ¾ hp pump for two jets, a 1 hp pump for three, a 1½ hp pump for four or five, and a 2 hp pump for six. Most manufacturers stay close to that formula.

Other variables are distance from pump to tub, and height water must be raised by the pump. Both diminish its flow capacity.

When the pump size changes, so does the filter. With a ¾ or 1 hp pump, the filter can be rated at 50 gallons per minute. A 1½ hp pump would call for a 70 gpm capacity, a 2 hp pump for 100 gpm.

Heaters are not directly related to flow rate. However, the number of jets and the presence or absence of a blower greatly affect their recovery time for lost heat.

Most heaters are chosen for their speed of heating. The 145,000 BTU heater in this hypothetical system would heat a 500-gallon tub from 50°F to 110°F (10°C to 43°C) in about 2 hours 15 minutes. A 12Kw (55,000 BTU) electric heater would need 5 hours, an 85,000 BTU tank heater 3 hours 45 minutes. On the other side, a 175,000 BTU coil heater would need 1 hour 30 minutes.

Of course start-up heating is a once or twice-a-year event. However, the figures index a major factor: flash heaters heat quickly, usually with one cycle just ahead of bathing. (Many are timed to work with the filter.) Tank heaters work off a thermostat, keeping water at bathing temperature at all times through repeat cycles.

System 2 adds a blower to the basic package. The blower has two effects: it speeds heat loss in the water, and it intensifies the sensation of moving water.

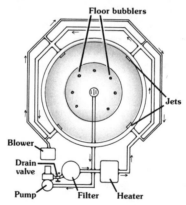

Consequently, it might call for one of the fast heaters, and at the same time allow a smaller pump than the basic chart suggests. One supplier, for example, says a ¾ hp pump is ample for four jets if there also is a blower pump hooked to them.

System 3 goes in reverse, toward a minimal cost and, with that, a minimal action in the water. It uses a ½ or ¾ hp pump linked only to the filter (and maybe one jet). The

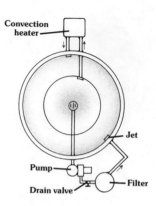

convection heater works on a separate loop without power from a pump.

System 4 is the same as System 1, except that it adds a chlorinator. These units fit between the inlet and outlet lines as shown so the disinfectant can mix thoroughly before entering the tub or spa.

Semi-automatic ones release a disinfectant into the water at a set rate. A gauge has to be set manually to adjust the flow to demand. Fully automatic models have a sensor which monitors demand and adjusts flow continuously.

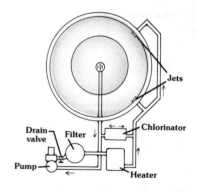

Other devices. Several smaller devices exist to make management of tubs and spas easier.

Automatic timers—24-hour clocks with adjustable on-off switches —automatically will run pump-and-filter systems on a daily cycle. Flash heaters can be tied in to these clocks. Tank and convection heaters must cycle more frequently, so operate on regular thermostats.

Insulation for pipes can be useful in cold winter regions. Insulation comes as a foam sleeve, or as wrap-around resistance-heated wire.

Sun-powered Tubs

Solar energy as a source of bill-free heat continues to grow in appeal and efficiency.

Solar is adaptable to hot tubs or spas. In sunny regions, it can do all the work nearly all the time. In less favored climates it still remains a money-saving element in the support system. Some states aid the payback potential with tax credits. (For example, California offers 55% of total solar parts and installation costs in tax credits.)

Initial cost of a full solar water heating system is high, from $2500 to $4500 by expert estimate. But when the sun is shining for more than 6 hours a day, these systems can provide from 70% to 100% of your tub or spa total water heating needs.

To accompany a solar heating system, most building codes typically require a conventional back up heating system. A large gas heater (over 100,000 BTUs) is usually recommended, since it will quickly bring your tub or spa water to temperature on cloudy days. Because of high electricity cost and long recovery times, electric heaters are not recommended as backups for solar heated units.

If you use your tub or spa infrequently it may take up to 10 years to earn back your original investment on solar equipment. But if you're an avid bather, you can cut recovery time down to as little as 18 months, and receive added pleasure from soaking in a tub or spa that is heated from the sun.

To be effective, the solar system must be designed, not along the lines of swimming pool installations, but much like those of domestic hot water systems. Both require high temperatures over 100°F (38°C).

The demands of an average-sized hot tub or spa require single or double-glazed liquid collector panels, tied into copper, polybutylene or CPVC piping. (Do not use unglazed PVC panels used for swimming pool heating; they will not produce the high water temperatures needed for hot tubs and spas.)

The Solar-assisted Tub or Spa

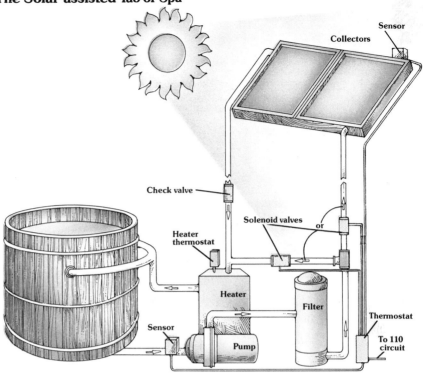

Estimates on needed collector surface vary from two 3 x 8 or 3 x 6 foot panels, up to 80 to 120 square feet, in three or four units, for a tub or spa 4 feet deep by 6 feet in diameter.

When not in use, always keep your solar heated tub or spa covered with an insulating blanket or lid. This turns the hot tub or spa into its own heat storage container, making an extra storage tank unnecessary.

Water flow rate controls the temperature of the water coming from the collectors to the hot tub or spa. A faster flow rate than used on domestic hot water systems keeps the water from scalding the bathers. In any case water temperature will not exceed that set in the spa controller thermometer.

There are a variety of ways to tie your tub or spa into the sun. Some homeowners choose to heat tub or spa water along with their household hot water (a double-wall heat exchanger separates the potable from the nonpotable water). Others decide to enclose their solar tub or spa in a solar greenhouse. Since variables abound, the accompanying sketch serves only as an explanation of the simplest solar system. For

more ideas and information on hot tub and spa solar related equipment, contact local solar companies versed in hot tub or spa installation, and see *Sunset's Homeowner's Guide to Solar Heating & Cooling.*

Tying Into a Pool

People who own swimming pools and are thinking about adding a tub or spa can save a considerable expense on installation costs by using all or part of the existing pool support equipment system to help pump, filter, and/or heat the tub or spa.

Before deciding to do this, determine the distance from pool equipment to the tub or spa, the size and type of the swimming pool lines, the size of the pool pump, and the pool heater size. Then ask a contractor or installer for advice about what part of the pool's support equipment should or can do double duty for your tub or spa.

Installation Tips

The notion of doing all installation work on a tub or spa has a certain fateful appeal to the handy. The idea of doing at least some of the work has a decided practical appeal to every budget-minded buyer of these costly systems, since savings can approach $1,000.

This section is only a guide to the size of the task—whole and parts—to help shape decisions about who should do which parts of the installing. Too many variables exist in equipment, and the jobs are too complex to describe in textbook detail. In fact, the installation guides of most manufacturers run more than 20 pages for any one model of tub or spa. Some suppliers also offer how-to classes.

Assumed in all of the following is that all proper building permits will be in hand. This is the best possible guarantee for a do-it-yourself installer that his design is both workable and safe, since permits require inspection of a detailed plan of the system before approval is granted for work to begin. It is a similar guarantee to the man who has hired a contractor that the work will be done according to code.

Installing a Wooden Hot Tub

The major tasks, in sequence, are to prepare a foundation for the tub and its support equipment, to assemble the tub and get it in place on its foundation, and to connect all elements of the support system to each other and the tub.

The Foundation

Reinforced concrete slabs are the preferred choice as the foundation for hot tubs. In some cases piers on concrete footings are suitable.

Slabs serve best because they work as a unit, so will not transmit stress to the tub if they shift. Piers on footings are sometimes the only way to get around disturbed topsoil; they can be suitable whenever the footings rest in stable soil.

Slabs. To bear a tub, a slab should be 4 inches thick, minimum, and reinforced with steel rods. Ideally, there will be footings at each corner and at the center.

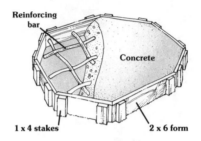

Reinforcing bar
Concrete
1 x 4 stakes
2 x 6 form

Slabs for support equipment can be poured at the same time. They need be only 3½ inches thick, and do not need reinforcement. Typically, 3 x 5-feet is big enough, but this should not be taken for granted.

The site should be skimmed or dug down to undisturbed earth, and made level. For maximum stability, the concrete should be underlain by 2 inches of sand.

Edge forms can be of 2 x 6, with 1 x 2 to 2 x 4 support stakes no more than 4 feet apart. The forms should be set with one side ½ to 1 inch lower than the other so the tub will tilt slightly for more efficient drainage. (Which is the low side will be governed by where the drained water is to go, and how.)

If any part of the perimeter of the slab is to be below grade, a curbing must be built up to avoid mud washing onto the slab. On a sloping site, the curbing may grow into a retaining wall, with its attendant requirements for extra drainage and footings.

This job should be timed so the slab can cure for 7 to 10 days before the tub is placed on it.

Piers and footings. Many builders resist this system because water draining or running under the tub may in time undermine footings, or otherwise cause uneven settling. Others insist that with proper footings the system is reliable.

Footings should be dug several inches into packed soil.

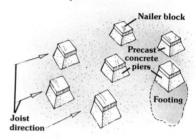

Nailer block
Precast concrete piers
Footing
Joist direction

The units must be placed on a pattern suggested by the supplier to assure even bearing ability, and to locate the joists inside the inner circumference of the staves.

Joists should be oriented so the drain line can run to the pump without elbows.

Pier tops should be level across the joists, and may be sloped ½ to 1 inch along the length of the joists for easier drainage of the tub.

Assembling the Tub

Although tubs can be bought assembled, most buyers get kits—tubs which have been precision-milled by the coopering firm.

The kit consists of floor joists, floor boards, staves, and metal hoops (plus, possibly, doweling for the floor, and seats).

Tools needed are a rubber mallet (or hammer and block of wood), hammer, a pair of wrenches, and perhaps a drill, a screwdriver, a hand plane and a jointer or table saw.

Supplies include nails to tack guides, sandpaper, and, if your supplier recommends it, mastic.

The job requires two able bodies.

If the tub site is a tight squeeze, assemble the tub in a more open spot; four people can carry it into place after it is whole more easily than it can be put together in cramped quarters.

Joists. Joists rest free on slabs. They are toe-nailed to pier blocks. On setting, they should be checked for level with each other, and for any slight lengthwise slope for drainage. If any correction is needed, shim under a joist, not on top.

Floor. Many kit sellers number the floor pieces sequentially. If there are no numbers, arrange the pieces with their beveled sides *down*.

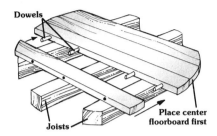

Dowels

Joists

Place center floorboard first

Some floors distribute weight loads laterally with tongue-and-groove. Some use a system of dowels.

Also, to reduce early leaking, some suppliers recommend a bead of mastic on the lower half of each joint as the pieces are fitted. (The mastic should not come close to the top of the joint; pressure could force it into the tub, where it would leach chemicals into the water.)

Floors must be placed so that the weak lower tips of the staves—the chines—do not rest on the joists. Check clearances before beginning to seat staves.

Start with the center floor board and work out. If not built on site, the floor should be carried to the site for a test fitting when complete. A floor sits with its boards at right angles to the joists. It is not nailed to them.

Staves. Correct spacing is crucial. Also crucial in the case of pre-drilled kits is correct relationship of drilled staves to location of support system AND to floor boards (since the latter must rest at right angles to joists).

Some kits number the staves. Those not drilled may not.

Many suppliers recommend scribing a line around the circumference of the floor equal to the

depth of the croze, the deep notch that holds staves in place. This line then shows when staves are fully seated.

The first stave is fitted so that it is centered on a joint in the floor, and driven half the depth of the croze. (Try not to seat any stave fully; tightening the hoops does that.) The assistant holds the top steady while the hammerer pounds.

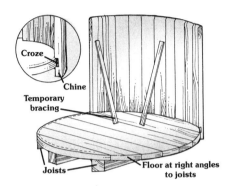

Croze

Chine

Temporary bracing

Joists

Floor at right angles to joists

Work clockwise, seating each stave half the depth of the croze, and tapping it so it seats snugly against its neighbor at the bottom. (Don't worry about the tops being out of line.) No stave joint should fall within ⅛-inch of a floor joint. If this happens, remove the stave, and work counterclockwise, so that the last two staves can be trimmed to avoid a double joint.

The last stave is where a payoff comes for keeping the kit warm and dry before construction. It will fit best if the wood is close to the same condition as when the tank left the cooperage.

If the last stave does not fit, it may need to be ripped. To do this, measure the gap at the inside and outside edges of the adjoining stave. Mark these measurements on the last stave. Trim to size and to angle using a jointer or table saw.

Hoops. The hoops go on last, starting with the bottom one. Most kits come with rolled steel hoops tightened by lugs.

Kit suppliers include a specific formula for spacing hoops, but the bottom one always is centered on the edge of the floor.

To hold hoops at proper levels, drive small nails at every seventh stave for each hoop.

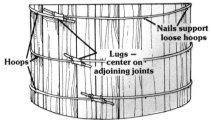

Nails support loose hoops

Hoops

Lugs — center on adjoining joints

It takes two to bend a hoop around a tank, and thread the last end into the lug. The first lug should be centered over a stave joint out of traffic patterns. The next lug should be on the opposite side of the tub over a joint. Each succeeding lug should center over another joint, working clockwise.

Once all hoops are in place, they should be tightened until just snug against the staves, which still are seated only half the depth of the croze. At this point, one man gets inside the tub with mallet (or hammer and block) while the other stays outside with the wrench.

The inside man hammers the staves while the outside man cinches up the hoops. Both are working to make edges of adjoining staves become flush as the tub moves toward perfectly round inside and outside surfaces.

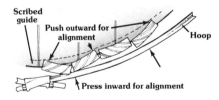

Scribed guide

Push outward for alignment

Hoop

Press inward for alignment

Work always starts with the bottom hoop and moves up. Typically there are four to six cycles of this before the staves are firmly seated. (A scribed line on the floor as shown above is the best guide.)

When the staves are set and the hoops tight, the tub is ready for its plumbing fittings and seats if the latter are to be built in. (Suppliers recommend stainless steel screws for anchoring seats.)

Installing a Spa

Installing a fiberglass shell spa is at once easier and harder than dealing with a wooden tub.

The tub requires a great deal of work, and in the end everything has to have been done just so. But there are ample chances along the way to tinker here and shove there in order for the final product to be right.

In working with a spa, there are many fewer steps because you start with one often unwieldy piece rather than forty or fifty. However, there are correspondingly few chances to correct mistakes. Nearly every step has to be made right the first time.

The sequence of steps is slightly different than for tubs. First comes site preparation. Then, however, the processes of setting the tub in its site and connecting the plumbing go forward in alternating stages rather than separately.

Required for the job:
2 x 4s and stakes for levelling framework, plus hammer and nails,
PVC pipe cutter and cement,
Sand (and, optionally, cement for the backfill).

Other materials should come as part of the kit. The instruction book may specify added tools.

Preparing the Site

Whether the spa is dug into the ground, or set above grade with the help of masonry or other solid walls, the first step is to develop a hole six inches deeper than the spa, and nine inches wider all around.

The more stable the earth surrounding this hole, the longer the spa will have solid support to keep it from cracking.

Trenches for plumbing should be dug at the same time. (Recall that the line from the drain to the pump should run continuously upslope, and that the suction line should have as few fittings or turns as possible.)

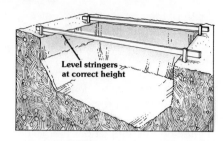

Level stringers at correct height

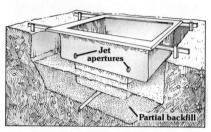

Jet apertures

Partial backfill

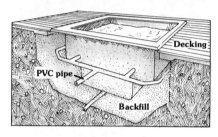

Decking

PVC pipe

Backfill

In establishing the depth of the excavation, remember that the lip of a fiberglass spa *will not bear weight.* It is designed to recess beneath surrounding decking or fit flush atop it.

Before setting the spa, drive stakes at four corners. Between these stakes, nail 2 x 4 stringers absolutely level. The spa will rest on these in correct final position as it is being set.

Setting the Spa

Once the spa is uncrated, the main drain and its water line is fitted. (In most shells, there are knockout holes for all fittings.)

All fittings are made the same way: a gasket is coated with sealant on both sides so that it adheres both to spa and fitting. Lock nuts, if any, are made finger tight, not tightened with a wrench. (The excess pressure could crush the shell, allowing a leak to start.)

After this is done, the spa is lifted into position on the stringers. If the drain line touches ground, the spa must be lifted back out and enough soil dug away to allow easy clearance.

Manufacturers differ on when to start backfilling. Some recommend placing the tub over the empty excavation, and backfilling under it. Others suggest putting a sand base down before positioning the tub. In the latter system, the tub is rocked in the sand to carve its own niche.

Some companies recommend using wet sand as the backfill. Others recommend a 4:1 mix of sand and cement. (The extra expense of the sand-cement mixture provides a more solid underpinning to the fiberglass shell, but neither system is an absolute guarantee against eventual erosion.)

In either case, the backfill must be packed tightly so that no air pockets remain. Backfilling proceeds only as far as any plumbing connections in the walls.

Once the set is assured as level and solid, the second tier of plumbing connections is made and pressure-tested as required by code. Then backfilling resumes to the desired final level. There is, obviously, enormous variation in the amount and complexity of plumbing, depending on the spa's shape, number of jets, and other variables.

The final step is to lay finished decking to the spa's edge.

Concrete Spas

Concrete is difficult to work with in most spa installations, no matter which of the following methods is considered.

Concrete block walls combined with a poured floor is the simplest system mechanically, but blocks cannot be set in curves of less than 10-foot diameter, too large for a typical spa. (Right angle corners are dirt catchers, to be avoided.)

Poured concrete using forms requires great ingenuity and great amounts of labor to build and set the forms, especially where they curve. (Some contractors build re-usable forms as an alternative to buying gunite equipment; they may be worth checking out if concrete is otherwise ideal.)

Hand-packed concrete must have sloping walls, which make entry into and exit from the spa difficult, and otherwise limit its shape.

Gunite, then, is the best adapted method for building a spa out of concrete because it may be shaped freely. There still remain two considerable difficulties: price, and the relative to absolute scarcity of contractors with the necessary equipment anywhere outside metropolitan markets.

The process is worth describing for those who can make a concrete spa economical by building it simultaneously with a gunite swimming pool.

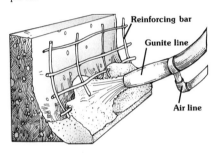

The excavation is dug to shape, then a gridwork of reinforcing rods is set.

Gunite, a mixture of hydrated cement and sand, is then applied over and under the reinforcing rods directly against the soil.

Application is from a transit mixer through a pressure nozzle. The mix is very dry. It must be applied at the proper thickness or weak spots may develop that are unable to resist earth and hydrostatic pressures. Also the gunite must be directed behind the rods and against the earth so that pockets of air or loose sand cannot form.

Plumbing must be roughed in ahead of time. All inlet and outlet openings should be covered with plastic so gunite does not clog them.

Gunite has a rough texture, and must be hand-trimmed before a finish coat of plaster or paint is applied. Finishers move in right behind the gunite crew to trim walls and floors, and to cut skimmer openings or any other openings.

Utility Hookups

By and large, utility hookups are the province of professionals. But do-it-yourselfers can help their budgets by paving the way for contractors and by doing some of the connecting work between tub or spa and support system.

Mostly paving the way means digging trenches for underground installations, or drilling holes for above-grade work when it has to get through existing walls.

Plumbing

Plumbing can mean iron, copper, or one of the plastics. There is usually some mixing of these materials.

Iron. Gas for heaters requires black iron. For water, galvanized pipe is used.

Galvanized is difficult to work with because cutting is slow, threading requires a special (though rentable) tool, and forming tight joints is exacting labor.

Its virtues are better resistance to freeze damage than plastic in severe climates, and general ability to withstand jolts.

Copper. Although expensive, it can be used for water. The tubing is moderately flexible, so may need fewer joints than iron. Soldered joints are quicker to make than iron.

A length of copper is required by many manufacturer warranties as a heat sink between heater and plastic pipe. (Its ability to exchange heat means it should be insulated in other uses.)

Plastic. PVC (polyvinyl chloride) is the commonest water pipe used in tub and spa work. Lightweight, easy to cut, easy to join (with special cements), it also is inexpensive compared to the other two.

Its greatest weakness is a tendency to crack easily with freezing. Check your local building code for any regulations regarding the use of PVC with heated water.

Flexible polyethylene tubing is particularly employed in short connections between units in the support system, where there may be large offsets in short distances.

Most codes require that all gas connections be made by licensed professionals. They may also require professional hookups to main water lines. However, do-it-yourselfers usually are free to plumb within recirculating systems for tubs.

Electrical Connections

The possible electrical connections in a tub or spa assembly are: primary pump(s), air pump for a bubbler, heater, spa light, and external illumination.

An electric heater requires a 230 volt circuit of its own from the master panel.

Most pumps should be wired at 230 volts, also on a separate circuit from the master panel. Some can be wired at 115 volts.

Blowers and lights usually are wired at 115 volts, and may fit into an existing circuit.

There cannot be more than a handful of Americans who have not been warned about keeping electric appliances well away from the bathtub while they are using it. Tub and spa owners are using electrical appliances to power a close relative to a bathtub. The need for extreme caution bears repeating.

All wiring must be done correctly, to exacting code requirements. Any failure may lead to a fatal accident. It is for this reason that almost all suppliers and manufacturers and many building codes, insist on professional hookups of electric-powered elements in support systems.

In addition to being wired from the master panel, pumps must have grounding for motor and frame alike, as must electric heaters. In addition, ground fault interrupters are required for both. Anyone not perfectly conversant with the techniques and devices for all such wiring and grounding should not attempt any part of it.

Buying Wisely

The hot tub and spa industry is new and growing fast. Automatically, the chance of making costly mistakes is greater than normal.

Burgeoning rosters of manufacturers, suppliers and contractors will have at least a few enthusiastic but inexperienced or inept members. Neither is the possibility of coming across a fast-buck artist remote enough to ignore.

Under the circumstances, it pays to take extra precautions not only in selecting materials, but in choosing suppliers and contractors.

Who Does What?

To repeat a point, installing an assembly that moves water under pressure requires skills from several trades.

Some companies act only as suppliers, as sellers of custom packages or kits. Others not only sell units, but contract as the installers.

A buyer planning to do much of his own work is well advised to choose a supplier with high-quality kits *and* a reservoir of information about installation.

Buyers who plan to have all of the work done should look either for a full-service tub or spa company, or for an independent contractor with a track record in pool or spa work. (Many supplier companies without installers of their own will recommend contractors.)

If there are several promising companies in the region, get bids from two or more competitors. The bid process will not only turn up the fairest price, it may expose weak points in equipment or services.

Check Out the Business

If a deal is to linger longer than cash-and-carry, buyers are well advised to check out financial stability in any company before signing any contracts.

If a firm goes out of business after signing, but before delivering, the loss may be the buyer's.

Longevity is one indicator of fiscal soundness. Bank or other credit references are surer.

If the company is to serve as installing contractor as well as supplier, inquire further.

A check with the state Contractor Licensing Board will show if the firm is licensed, bonded, and insured for workman's compensation. These are your best—essentially only—guarantees against legal and/or financial troubles if something goes wrong with a company or its work.

Under the laws of most states, a creditor of a contractor may file liens against the company's current work. In short, money you owe the contractor by contract may be taken legally by the contractor's creditor as payment against debt. (Such liens are limited to debts for materials used on your property and labor performed there.)

The bond is at least partial protection against such an eventuality. (A bond is an amount of money deposited with the state licensing agency against possible claims.) Many contractors post only minimum required bond. Claims beyond this value still may be filed against the contractor's clients.

There is a limited time for filing such claims. Known as the lien period, the time usually is 30 to 60 days after completion of a job. Most states offer additional legal protection to individuals against liens. Inquire of the Contractor Licensing Board at the same time you check on candidate contractors.

References and Referrals

Reputable, experienced companies are willing to provide references, or referrals to completed installations.

Newer installations show how well done is current work, and may give some useful hints about prices. Older work is an index of durability in materials, and in quality of follow-up service.

In addition to checking with former customers, it is prudent to inquire at non-profit watchdog organizations. Better Business Bureau and other general consumer protection agencies can help with credit and performance checks. The International Association of Plumbing and Mechanical Officials (5032 Alhambra Ave., Los Angeles 90032) will provide quality assessments of proposed equipment.

There is something of Catch 22 in all this for new companies. They miss out on jobs for lack of experience, and get no experience because they miss out on jobs. Buyers who do not mind gambling may be able to secure favorable contracts from new firms.

Writing Contracts

Every agreement between buyer and seller should appear in a final written contract. A good contract will include:
- *A completion date.*
- *A complete listing of equipment and services.* The list of equipment should include names of manufacturers and model numbers of all major elements, and quality designations for pipes, fittings, and minor pieces, plus agreed prices for all items shown. The list of services should specify who is to perform each part of the work, and show a firm estimate on price for each aspect.
- *All guarantees and warranties.* These must include work guarantees or warranties and equipment guarantees. Manufacturers' guarantees should be appended along with those of the seller and installing contractor. Lengths of all guarantees should be specified. Work guarantees should specify on-site service.
- *Terms of delivery.*
- *Payment schedule.* An ideal contract would provide for payment in no less than three stages: down payment, completion payment, and final payment at the end of any lien period.
- *Servicing Policy.* The installing contractor should make specific commitments about what follow-up service will be available. (This may be refused by a general contractor rather than a specialist in tub and spa work. In this case, the buyer is forewarned to find a separate service organization.)

Getting Launched

For those who take the plunge, the day finally comes when a tub or spa is no longer a plan, but a reality.

The remainder of this section deals with that time, which may not begin as smoothly as one could hope.

New tubs leak and discolor water. Both spas and tubs turn water cloudy for a time after installation. Curing and conditioning programs take a week, sometimes a few days longer.

Preparing a Tub

The first job is to get the tub swelled tight so water will stay in it long enough to be treated.

For the first filling, use a hose with a lawn sprinkler set so that staves are wet from the top down while the tub fills. This will start the staves swelling some hours before they have to hold the full weight of the water.

If a leak turns to a gusher, the staves have been milled poorly, or spaced incorrectly. Poor milling should be visible to the eye, and should be returned to the supplier. More likely, the question is poor spacing. Be glad if an installer has to fix his own mistake. If you did your own work, the first step is to loosen lug nuts on the hoops one turn, no more than two. Then, using a rubber mallet (or a hammer and a protective block) pound on the bottom hoop in an effort to adjust stave spacing, or seat the staves tighter, or both. Begin at the point opposite the leak and work back to it around *both* sides. Work about two staves on one side, then switch to the other. Alternate sides all the way around. When the circle is complete, retighten the lugs only until they are hard to turn.

This process may have to be repeated several times.

Do not try to cure a fast leak only by tightening the hoops. Above all, do not force the tightening. It will only increase uneven pressures if a stave is out of alignment.

If early leaks are slow seepers, do not hurry to do anything. Most will stop within the first week.

Persistent slow leaks will need caulking.

A simple, practical caulk is cotton string wedged between staves with a butter knife or other dull blade.

There are differences of opinion about whether string caulking should be applied from the inside or the outside when leaks are between staves. The argument for caulking outside is that the caulk can be inserted directly at the leak. (In wineries, this is how the work is done, but there is a practical reason; the inner walls are covered with tartrate crystals, so joints are hard to work.) The argument for caulking inside is that pressure moves that way, so the caulk will be pushed in—while outside caulking might be forced out. This is the same general theory as caulking on the water side of a boat hull.

If there is a leak at the joint between floor and staves, the caulk goes inside, no questions allowed. This is, incidentally, the commonest point of leakage.

Another effective material is the plastic marine putty used to caulk boat hulls. This is applied only to the outside.

If a stave leaks through a weak spot right in its middle, let the tub drain below the leak. After the spot dries, paint a generous patch with exterior polyurethane varnish. Clear is best. It shows least, and lets you keep an eye on the spot. Again caulk on the outside.

New redwood will turn water a fairly dark tea-color. The color source in tea and redwood is tannin. Its presence is absolutely harmless. However, few people can accustom themselves to bathing in tea.

The least damaging cure as far as the tub is concerned is frequent draining and refilling coupled with 2 to 3 hours of filtering daily.

(Many dealers recommend letting the first tubful darken and draining it away without turning on the filter. The heavy tannin content stains and clogs the filter. Thereafter you get a day or two of clear water with each refilling, so can use the tub while the tannins leach.)

Another aid is regular use of a water clarifier, which helps precipitate the tannins in the filter. It also is possible to keep the disinfectant higher than normal through a chlorination every other day (see page 29), although this is hard on the interior surface and the support machinery.

Some dealers have recommended dumping 2 pounds of soda ash per 1,000 gallons of water into the tub during its first filling. This does leach pigments rapidly, but also is harmful to the interior surface in far greater degree than is extra chlorination. Most dealers now recommend against the practice.

Preparing a Fiberglass Spa

Although spas do not have startup leaks, and do not leach tannins, residual dusts and dirt from installation do need to be eliminated before the water will be clear and clean looking.

Run filters for 2 to 4 hours daily for the first week. Use spa water clarifiers twice a week, and chlorinate more often than will be normal once the spa is in established operation.

Preparing a Gunite Spa

The plaster linings in gunite spas need special treatment during their first months in operation.

Extended filtration is the safest way to clear water. Avoid heavy chlorination for at least a month. Do not add acid for this period, as acid can etch plaster easily until it has cured. (During this time, pH should be maintained at 7.4 and up.)

Starting Up the Machinery

Manufacturers' instructions should be read and understood in every particular before turning on any part of the mechanical support system.

Two points are absolute musts:
• Air must be bled from the pump-filter system, which is to say it must be perfectly primed.
• Water must fill the heater before it is turned on.

Maintaining Your Investment

A smart buy is the right way to begin ownership of a tub or spa, but a diligent maintenance program is the only way to enjoy having one.

Maintenance comes in three parts. The most frequent and most vital task is keeping the water clean and in chemical balance. This not only makes the bath itself more pleasurable, it minimizes the other two phases of maintenance—keeping tub or spa surfaces clean, and keeping pumps, filters and heaters clean and in good working order.

Keeping Water Clean

If tranquility is a major reason for getting into a tub or spa, clouds of algae settling on one's skin spoil the effect. More important, clouds of invisible bacteria tend to go with algae, and, in hot water, human skin is especially open to infection.

As for equipment, excessive solids in water place strains on pump and filter. Also unbalanced water may corrode metal in the plumbing system wherever the two come in contact, or may damage the surface of either tub or spa.

Most of the above thoughts are familiar to swimming pool owners. However, the need to maintain water in good condition in tubs and spas is more critical than for swimming pools.

The ratio of bathers to water volume is likely to be much closer than in swimming pools. It is not uncommon to have five people in a 500- to 700-gallon tub or spa. To achieve an equal density of people in a typical 25,000-gallon swimming pool would call for a mob of 200 to 250. The amounts of body oils, hair, and dirt that must be pumped into the filter and trapped are similarly proportionate.

Water temperatures are higher, up to a recommended maximum of 100°F in a typical tub as opposed to 69° to 85°F (20° to 29°C) in an average swimming pool. Quick, high heating means a small volume of water must make several passes through the pump-filter-heater system for each pass in a swimming pool system.

Higher temperatures combined with bubbles not only invite growth of bacteria and algae, they also lead to more rapid breakdown of disinfectants used to inhibit such growth. Another upshot of high temperatures is build-up of mineral scale. (Evaporation concentrates minerals.)

Still, important as water maintenance is, it is not difficult.

The first line of defense is the filter. In a typical system, it should run 2 to 3 hours per day. (It must be kept clean itself. See page 31.)

The key, though, is having a test kit and using it often, so water always can be kept close to optimum condition. Frequent small adjustments are wiser than rare major corrections.

A kit should be able to test:
• pH
• total alkalinity
• chlorine or bromine
• water hardness

At publication, test kits ranged in price from $3 to $50. The higher-priced ones usually include several months' supply of corrective chemicals.

Since different kits may use somewhat differing tests, it is vital to follow directions precisely for each test.

How and When to Correct

Some people drain and refill their tubs or spas frequently to minimize chemical correction of water balance. Many experts feel this approach best preserves equipment.

Although used water may be used safely to irrigate gardens, frequent replacement may be an ecological luxury some water-short owners cannot afford. In any case, nearly every tub or spa will need at least some chemical treatment of its waters.

Most owners use the chemicals familiar from swimming pool maintenance. Again, it must be emphasized that spas and tubs are not swimming pools. They differ in size, water temperature, water aeration, and construction materials, so chemicals must be chosen and used somewhat differently.

The roster of essential chemicals is:
• a disinfectant—bromine or chlorine
• an alkaline, usually soda ash, to rebalance too-acidic water
• acid, to rebalance too-alkaline water
• spa water clarifier to coagulate microscopic solids so they can be trapped by the filter.

Useful—sometimes essential—supplements are:
• Water softener as a guard against staining and mineral scale
• A specific algaecide where algae are too stubborn for bromine or chlorine
• An anti-foam agent to rid water of suds.

Because tubs and spas differ so widely in materials and rate of use, and because water varies so widely in chemical makeup, no specific program of maintenance exists. Each owner must develop his own schedule.

A disinfectant is the most frequent addition, and one of the easiest to manage. But the real basis of good quality water is correct pH. Its function must be understood first.

pH (potential Hydrogen). The pH of water is a measure of its acid/alkaline balance.

The pH scale ranges from 0 to 14, with 7 being neutral, 0 to less than 7 acidic, and more than 7 to 14 alkaline.

Proper pH in tub or spa water is in the range 7.2 to 7.8.

Above 7.8, water is too alkaline, and should be corrected by adding an acid. Water too high in pH may:
• greatly reduce efficiency of the disinfectant as a deterrent to algae and bacteria growth
• allow water to grow hazy

• allow formation of mineral scale on tub or spa surface and in support equipment
• allow filter to clog.

Below 7.2, water is too acidic, and should be corrected by adding an alkaline. Water too low in pH may:
• cause eye burn or skin irritation.
• etch a spa finish, or cause breakdown in cell walls of wooden tubs
• corrode metal parts in the support system.

The test should be made every second or third day at the same time you test for disinfectant.

Correcting alkalinity. Far and away the commonest alkaline used in tubs and spas is soda ash, although it usually comes compounded with other materials in a patented or trade-marked formula. (This is true of other chemicals as well, but their basic ingredients are more familiar.)

Measuring pH does not give total acid or alkaline content of water, only the balance between the two, so water should be tested for alkalinity once a month, or whenever high pH persists. (When alkalinity is correct, pH usually is correct, too.) The acceptable range is 90 to 180 parts per million.

If alkalinity falls below 100 ppm, add soda ash or another recommended alkaline as recommended by its manufacturer, or, if your local water supply permits, correct by partially draining and refilling the tub or spa.

Contrarily, if testing shows alkalinity exceeding 150 ppm, the pH may be too high. Correct as noted below.

Correcting acidity. Because testing for acid is relatively difficult, most tub and spa owners test for pH, then correct according to a table provided on the acid's package.

A majority of dealers recommend dry acids for use in tubs and spas. Even these, the easiest types to use, should be handled with real caution to avoid burned skin or clothing, or

damage to tub or spa surfaces. The recommended method is to dissolve a maximum of 1 ounce of acid into 2 gallons or more of water in a bucket, then to add this mixture to the main body of water slowly by partially submerging the bucket in the tub or spa well away from walls.

Throughout, the pump should be shut *off* to avoid concentrated acid passing through pump and filter.

Once the dilute acid is added, it should be mixed thoroughly before turning on the pump-filter-heater system. A separate blower will mix the fluids quickly. If the tub or spa has none use a long stick or paddle.

Swimming pool owners may be used to using liquid muriatic acid to condition water. For the same reasons that liquid chlorine is not recommended for tubs and fiberglass spas, neither is muriatic. It splashes, so can cause burns. Concentrated, it can etch some spa walls (especially those with gelcoat finishes), or can break down wood fiber in tubs.

If used, it should be diluted and floated into the tub or spa with even greater care than used with dry acids.

The warning cannot be repeated too often: allow at least an hour between additions of acid and chlorine to a tub or spa, to avoid risk of violent interaction between the two chemicals.

Disinfectants. Chlorine is the chemical disinfectant most often used to combat bacteria and algae in water—from municipal supplies to swimming pools to tubs and spas. Bromine is becoming an increasingly important alternative for tubs and spas.

Measured with a test kit, either should be between 1.0 and 2.0 parts per million in tub or spa water when it is to be used. Below 1.0 they are ineffective. Above 4.0, they irritate eyes and skin. Prolonged exposure to excess chlorine can corrode metal in the plumbing, and damage some spa and tub surfaces.

The test should be made every second or third day. A test for free available disinfectant is most accurate. Testing for residual disinfectant is adequate.

Most tubs and spa owners test for both disinfectant and pH, then

correct the disinfectant first.

A much-used maintenance program calls for moderate correction whenever the disinfectant is low, and a major addition every other week. The small corrections bring the level to 2.0 or just over. The heavy dose brings the level as high as 6.0 (but never should use more than twice the recommended daily dosage; chlorines are bleaches and excesses can cause damage).

Do not run the pump while the disinfectant is being added, or, in the case of heavy doses, until the test level drops back into the 2.0–4.0 ppm range. Usually this requires about an hour.

For minimum dissipation of disinfectant, add it at the end of a day, when the heater will not be used for some hours.

Bromine comes as tablets for use in chlorinators, or it comes as two dry chemicals which, when added to the water together, mix to make bromine in the tub or spa.

It is slightly more expensive than chlorine. Its manufacturers say it is a more effective disinfectant than chlorine in water with high concentrations of organic material.

Chlorine comes in liquid, granulated and tablet forms.

Most recommended is a dry, stabilized form. As granules, this type dissolves with little effect on water's pH. ("Stabilized" means it is treated to minimize loss due to ultra-violet sunlight.)

As in the case of acids, recommended practice is to dissolve granular chlorine into 2 gallons or more of water, and to introduce the dilute mixture into the tub or spa by partially submerging its container well away from the walls.

Chlorine in tablet form is used with chlorinators in the same way as bromine. (See page 20 for descriptions of these devices.)

Most dealers recommend against liquid chlorine in tubs and spas because it is the most caustic form and thus hard to introduce into small volumes of water without risking damage to surfaces.

Not recommended are trichlor and calcium hypochlorite. Trichlor is too acidic for tub or spa use. With a pH of 2.6 to 3.0 it is likely to damage tub or spa finish. The highly alkaline calcium hypochlorite may promote mineral scale in tub or spa and support equipment.

Water hardness. Hard water has excess mineral content, especially of calcium and magnesium.

The basic mineral content of water is extremely variable from region to region. But whatever the initial content, it will increase as water in a tub or spa evaporates (owing to heat, wind) and is replaced.

Water hardness is the final index for when to replace old water with new. Without addition of a water softener, or stain and scale preventative, the maximum level is 350 to 400 parts per million. With the addition of a softener, the count can go as high as 1000 ppm.

A single filling can be made to last from 1 to 4 months if the water is kept clean and in proper balance.

Using Chemicals Safely

Chemicals used in tub and spa maintenance are concentrated enough to be damaging if misused. Some may explode or generate dangerous gases if mixed together. Always take the following precautions in handling and storing chemical supplies.

• Do not mix different chemicals together. Even two different types of chlorine may react violently when mixed.

• Add chemicals to water when diluting. Pouring water onto chemicals may cause violent reactions.

• Add chemicals to water separately. There should be at least a one hour interval between additions of chlorine and acid. Minimum

interval between any two chemicals is 10 minutes.

• Do not get acid on skin or clothes. Dilute first, then add it to tub or spa water slowly, without splashing.

• Do not add chemicals to tub or spa while pump is running. Until thoroughly mixed into the water, chemicals can corrode support system. (Blowers can be turned on to help mix chemicals.)

• Keep all chemicals in a locked area out of reach of children. The area should be cool and dry.

• Do not store chemicals in an enclosed space with pumps, filters, or other support equipment. Chemicals emit corrosive fumes.

• Always read labels before using. Many packages are similar enough to be confused one with another at a glance.

• Wash with soap and water after mixing chemicals and adding them to spa or tub.

Maintaining Wooden Tubs

Wooden hot tubs require somewhat greater care than spas because wood is softer, more porous, and so more subject to unwanted changes in shape and texture.

• Keep the tub watertight. Once wood has swelled tight, a tub never should go empty more than two days. During long periods of disuse in wet seasons, it need not be kept full, but should not dip much below half. In hot, dry periods it should be kept full.

Allowed to dry, wood will shrink, and perhaps twist. Leaks stemming from prolonged or repeated drying are difficult if not impossible to cure.

• Preserve the exterior finish. Water, chemicals and weather can damage the outside walls. Two to four times a year, apply exterior Danish oil, or thinned linseed oil.

Sealers *never* should be applied to the interior surface, which must remain open-pored so water can penetrate and keep staves swollen tight together.

• Keep the interior clean and smooth through regular, careful maintenance of water condition (see page 28).

• Every few months give the tub a complete scrubbing with garden hose and brushes.

After draining, hose out the interior, taking care to wash nooks and crannies around seats, valves, and between staves.

• Watch for any signs of white, hair-like strands on the interior. Prolonged exposure to excess chlorine or to too-acidic water will cause breakdown of cell wall material (lignite), the source of the fuzzy look.

If this condition appears, the tub must be drained, allowed to dry for a day, then sanded smooth, first with an orbital sander, then by hand.

Once corrected, the process can be kept under control through careful maintenance of water quality.

• Protect metal hoops against rust or corrosion through periodic renewal of preservative oil or rust-inhibitor paint.

• Watch for late-blooming leaks. If these appear between staves or floor boards, check first for stress from uneven underpinnings. If the tub is seated squarely, caulk the leak as described on page 27.

If caulking does not stop the leak, check with the installer or supplier.

Maintaining Fiberglass Spas

Mineral scale, stains, and algae at the water line are the major maintenance headache for owners of these spas.

Proper water condition is the prime defense. It is especially worthwhile to keep water hardness at a low level through frequent draining and regular use of a recommended water softener.

Keep a brush handy to wipe away stain or algae at the water line whenever it is noticeable.

Drain the tub at least every two months for a thorough cleaning. First brush off any scale, dirt, or algae. Then use a non-abrasive powder or liquid detergent and scrub down entire spa.

If there is a tile band, make a weak solution of muriatic acid (1 part acid to 10 parts water), and wash the tile with this. Use a soft cloth or brush, and wear rubber gloves. Do not use swimming pool tile cleaners. These suds too much for a spa to handle.

When the cleaning is finished, hose out the interior thoroughly before refilling.

Twice a year, or whenever the interior begins to look dull or faded, give it a coat of a special wax available at spa suppliers.

If cracks or blisters appear in the spa finish, contact the firm which sold you the unit. Repairs are a professional's job.

Maintaining Concrete Spas

Concrete spas—almost always gunite—like hard-coated fiberglass shells, tend to stain and accumulate algae at the water line. However, treatment is different.

The best cleanser is the same weak solution (1:10) of muriatic acid used to clean tile.

Acid should not be used during the first three or four months after the spa is installed. The plaster finish must have time to cure, or acid may etch it.

Mechanical Maintenance

The three major elements in tub or spa support systems—filter, heater and pump—all require regular maintenance.

The filter demands most care of the three, the pump least.

It is worth extra effort to get maintenance manuals for all three units if they do not come with the original package, because specifics vary widely, and incorrect maintenance can be more damaging than none at all in some cases.

General requirements are as follows:

Filters

Diatomaceous Earth and sand filters both are cleaned by backwashing—reversing the water flow. Cartridge filters are removed, scrubbed, and replaced.

These periodic cleanings may come at variable intervals, depending on basic capacity, on how much use the tub or spa is getting, or how much plant material or other solid is getting into the water.

On average, filters need cleaning once a month.

Most filters have a pressure gauge. When this gauge shows pressure readings 5 to 10 pounds above normal, the filter is dirty or clogged enough to require cleaning, no matter what the interval.

Diatomaceous Earth filters. Backwashing a D.E. filter results in loss of the filtering material. This should be replaced after cleaning.

If a D.E. filter persistently needs cleaning, the plate against which the D.E. presses likely is clogged. This requires removing the D.E. and cleaning the unit by hand. If unfamiliar with this job, consult a pool cleaning company.

Backwashing loses a large amount of water. Some D.E. units have lift-out filters for easy washing.

Sand filters. Backwashing seldom results in loss of sand, a permanent medium.

If a sand filter persistently needs cleaning, the sand may need washing, a job for a pool cleaning company.

Cartridge filters. Cartridges pull out of the filter housing for hosing off and brushing. After, be sure to replace the filter correctly, so water flow is not restricted, and to secure the housing lid tightly.

Cartridges last 1 to 2 years, then must be replaced.

Heaters

The most common maintenance required for heaters—especially direct systems—is removing scale or mineral deposits from the heating elements.

Failure to do this reduces heating efficiency, and also may shorten the life of the heater.

In most areas, annual inspection is enough. In regions with hard water, heaters should be checked for scale twice a year.

Scale can be inhibited by using a stain and scale preventative, and by changing the water before mineral content builds beyond a desirable level (see page 30).

Pumps and Motors

Pumps and motors require almost no maintenance on the part of tub or spa owners. They do require careful watching to see that prime is not lost.

A pump operating dry—that is, with large amounts of air in the chamber—may damage its water seal. Pumps with plastic housings may even melt through over-heating.

If a pump does lose prime, stop the motor, fill the pump with water at the leaf strainer basket, replace the lid tightly, and restart.

The leaf strainer basket, incidentally, should be removed and emptied of debris every other week at least, weekly when leaves or other plant materials are falling steadily. Always check for prime before closing the lid.

A handful of pump motors still require lubrication. Manufacturer's booklets will specify intervals and types of lubricant.

A Hot Tub, Spa, and Sauna Gallery

- **Large lots**
- **Indoor rooms**
- **Entertainment areas**
- **Low-level decks**
- **Swimming pools**
- **Natural settings**
- **Little-used spaces**
- **The home health center**
- **Free-standing saunas**
- **Small-space saunas**

The Japanese refined the hot soak into an art form; the Finns developed the sauna into a way of life. But it was the Chinese who claimed that a picture is worth a thousand words, and that bit of wisdom sets the pace for the content of this hot tub, spa, and sauna gallery.

Here you will see photographs of many successful, modern installations, each offering a wealth of ideas adaptable to your own situation. Whatever your needs or desires, you're bound to find much to pique your curiosity and inspire your efforts.

Thumb through the pages of this gallery. Feast your eyes on the photographs and study the plans. Find out what installations appeal to you, and imagine how they might be modified to meet your own requirements. Remember, the key word here is "successful." These installations work for their owner. The proper adaptations can work for you.

***Classical and contemporary**
Japanese wooden tub shown at upper
left, facing page—filled from water
heater through oversized pipe—is used
strictly for soaking. (Design: Arthur
Hanna.) Fiberglass spa has hydro jets,
air bubblers, and its own heater, for full
therapeutic action; adjacent sauna
provides dry heat (for another view,
turn to page 54, lower right).*

Japanese-style tub house nestles in quiet corner of garden near end of koi pond (see plan below). Except for ¼ by 2-inch pine lattice, which conceals support equipment, tub house construction is cedar throughout. Translucent fiberglass windows, resembling shoji screens, are hinged at top; owners prop them open for fresh air and view of garden. Design: Donn Foster and Paul Bickler.

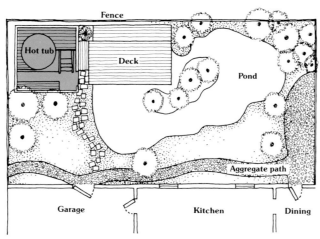

If you have a large lot . . .

A Japanese Hot-tub House for Privacy and Solitude

In Japan the wooden hot tub traditionally has been a retreat for relaxing the mind rather than a bath for cleansing the body. Separated from the main living quarters, it was housed in a simple structure that shielded it from curious eyes. Only the immediate family and honored guests partook in the hot bath ritual, which often included tea drinking and a leisurely stroll through the garden.

Today, many Western homeowners with outdoor space to spare have adapted this Eastern idea, some constructing an entire garden in classical Japanese style. Shown here are two fine examples of the Japanese hot-tub house, American-style.

Cedar tub—4 feet in diameter, 5 feet deep—rests on concrete pad. Entering tub house, owners step down to disrobing area, then climb short ladder to platform surrounding two-thirds of tub.

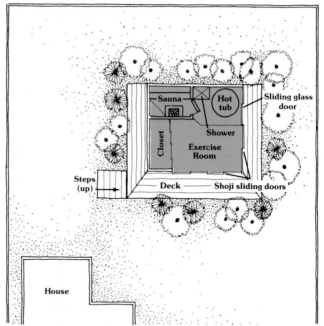

Half-sunken redwood tub, *6 feet in diameter, 4 feet deep, is in windowed corner of room. Entire garden house, including hot tub, exercise area, shower, and sauna (see plan below), was designed and built as a single project.*

In the plan:
- Sauna
- Hot tub
- Sliding glass door
- Closet
- Shower
- Exercise Room
- Steps (up)
- Deck
- Shoji sliding doors
- House

Hot-tub house *sits behind and slightly uphill of main house. Even on foggy days, owners enjoy a hot soak with shoji screens open. On clear days ". . . the view is magnificent, especially when we enjoy it from the tub." Design: Dolphin Woodworks and Maroto Imai.*

If you can set aside space indoors . . .

A Special Room for the Spa or Hot Tub

Wanting a hot soak handy to their living quarters, the owners of the two installations shown on this page managed to create space for it indoors. One added a compact hot-tub room as part of a second-story bathroom remodel; the other expanded the house at ground level, building a spacious spa room off the master bedroom.

Both hot-bath rooms have several windows for brightening the long soak and admitting fresh air for ventilation (a must in a steamy environment). Both rooms have tile floors to drain away splashed water and to make cleaning easier.

Fiberglass spa *is centered in slip-proof tiled floor of its own room. Accessible from living room and master bedroom (see plan at right), spa room has cedar walls, opening windows, two large skylights. Custom-designed light fixtures on walls give soft glow at night. Spa's support equipment is located in basement. Design: Gary Palmer.*

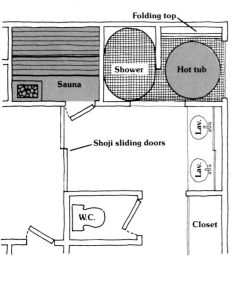

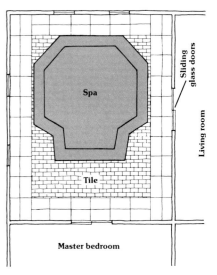

Cozy corner *of second-story bathroom (see plan at left) contains compact redwood tub installed above galvanized metal pan that drains overflow into household plumbing waste line. Support equipment is housed in a closet below tub on first floor. Design: Doug Zuberbuhler.*

An entertainment extension
for the house

A Hot-tub Socializing Area for Family and Friends

It's bound to happen! Desiring your place in the sun, you site your spa or hot tub outdoors, and in no time at all it becomes more than a watering spot. You and your family may use it strictly for soaking, but when friends come over it becomes a gathering place, a full-blown entertainment center.

Size doesn't matter. One of the installations shown on this page is sunk into the ground of a modest-sized patio. The other is part of a grand complex of decks, steps, and benches. Both are near the house, which means foot traffic can move freely from indoors to outdoors.

Whether for an intimate group or a large gathering, whether people are steaming in the water or standing around the tub's edge, the outdoor hot bath is a natural nucleus for socializing.

Outdoor entertaining area *centers around commodious (6 feet in diameter, 5 feet deep) redwood tub. Its interior benches are located to take advantage of ten jets arranged in pairs. Gas-fired heater, pump, and filter are housed under deck, close to tub. Design: Roger Somers.*

Near entertaining area, *redwood hot tub (a 6 by 8-foot oval, 4 feet deep) is set below grade in concrete vault sunk in brick patio floor. A course of ceramic tile—held by a special epoxy adhesive—is inset flush with the redwood around tub's top. Tub's support equipment is located nearby in small brick structure that looks like a decorative wall. Design: Malibu Spa.*

Rectangular hot tub, complementing planes and angles of contemporary house, is handy to master bath (see plan at right). Lattice gives privacy and baffles afternoon winds; large mirror inset in wall at end of deck reflects cityscape. Wrapping around three sides of house, generous deck extends outdoor living space. Design: California Redwood Spa.

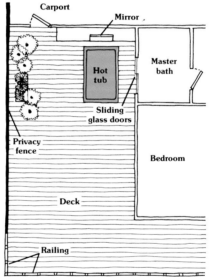

Outdoors, but close to the house

Four Hot Tubs, Just a Step Away from the Living Quarters

"We use our spa every night, to relax before bedtime," said one homeowner, "so it just had to be close to our bedroom."

"We could have put our hot tub out in the south forty," said another, "but since we always shower before we soak, we kept it handy to a bathroom."

Whether the hot tub is part of a new home construction or part of a remodel, keeping it close to the house makes good sense. First there's the convenience of stepping from house to hot bath. Then there's the economics: Installation close to the house means shorter plumbing and electrical lines.

Circular redwood hot tub is fitted into corner of deck off first-floor study (see plan at left) of hillside home in wooded setting. Trees and free-form privacy fence shield soakers. A wooden housing at end of deck contains support equipment. Design: Colorado Hot Tub Co.

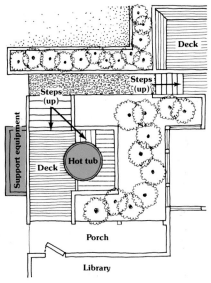

Accessible to library, *6-foot-diameter, 4-foot-deep redwood tub nestles in deck tucked into a small side yard (see plan above). Owners make year-round use of tub, which has fine view and is protected from breezes by house and plantings. Design: Bennett, Johnson, Slenes, and Smith.*

Opening off family room, *two-level cedar deck surrounds redwood tub resting on 4-inch concrete slab. Shingled wall behind tub provides privacy and helps hide support equipment (see plan at left). Semicircular wooden tub covers stand against wall. Design: Robert C. and Janet Slenes.*

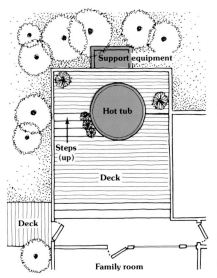

Close to the House **39**

Spas and Tubs As Part of a Landscaping Scheme

Many homeowners who particularly enjoy their gardens think of a hot tub or spa as a definite design element, an integral part of the overall landscaping scheme. Its size is manageable in almost any size lot; its shape—whether round, oval, rectangular, or hexagonal—lends itself to almost any landscaping situation.

A spa or hot tub "works" nicely with wood, masonry, natural rock, and plantings to create an integrated whole. So well do they work that many a homeowner, in adding on to a home, has restructured an entire back lot around a hot bath to gain a new multi-use outdoor living area.

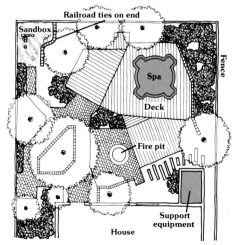

Integrated look *is given tiered suburban garden by multilevel decks, recycled-brick walks, railroad-tie dividers, and plantings—many of them in easily movable containers. Fiberglass spa was added and entire back yard redesigned into a multi-use outdoor living area when owners remodeled house. Design: R. Bottomley and Associates, Inc.*

Country-home owners *wanted oval hot tub installation to be near house and part of a total landscaping scheme. Accessible from den, main deck— 1 foot above grade— is outdoor sunning and dining area; raised platform at tub-top level provides handy space for towels, plants. Support equipment in house basement is connected by underground wiring and plumbing. Design: Holly and Charles Brumder.*

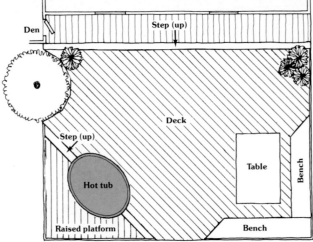

...a total landscaping scheme

Hot soak and cold plunge are provided by two pools that also form major landscaping elements in large rural garden. Upper-level gunite pond is heated only by sun, and its overflow runs through a trough to wooden tub several feet lower. Tub water is heated and recirculated; cold-pond overflow can be shut off from hot tub. Design: Carl Swenson.

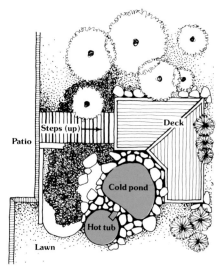

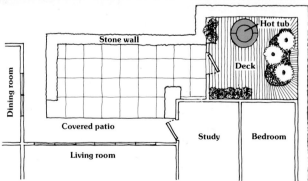

Small, enclosed garden, where redwood hot tub is sited just inside arched doorway in stone wall, extends house's Mediterranean architectural theme. Tub is accessible by a short stroll through patio. Housing for support equipment is on other side of wall. Design: Howdy King.

Part of the Landscape **43**

The subtle touch

These Hot Tubs Nestle in Low-level Decks

Don't want your hot tub to look like a free-standing barrel? Want it to make a subtle statement? One way to visually quiet down the strong lines of a hot tub is to sink it in a low-level deck. With the tub covered, you're hardly aware it's there.

Integrating hot tub and decking takes considerable planning—you don't just cut a hole in a deck and drop in the tub. Usually you begin with the tub, working out from it for the entire landscaping scheme and designing decking on several levels.

Modest-sized redwood deck, measuring only 10 by 14 feet, was designed to hold hot tub and to fit into a small side yard off guest bedroom and bath. Redwood tub, 6 feet in diameter, 4 feet deep, has eight jets and three benches at different levels. Turned-wood grabposts help tubbers get in and out of water easily. Design: Donald G. Boos.

Concrete patio was already there; so was the venerable Japanese black pine (at left). Owners wanted to keep both, but they also preferred a more natural look—and they desired a hot tub. The answer was to put a redwood tub on a new concrete pad and a redwood deck right over the old concrete, leaving an opening in the deck for the pine. And while they were at it, they added benches and a table for outdoor living. Design: Ed Hoiland.

Ground-level deck *shown below encloses a custom-designed redwood tub resting in an underground insulated room that houses heater, pump, and filter. Tub was 6 feet deep, but some of its staves were cut flush with deck surface; others create privacy areas and backrests for tubbers. The bronze bird is a water valve handle. Design: Steve Moeller.*

Circular redwood tub *shown above sits entirely beneath ground-level deck. The 5 by 5-foot tub was wrapped in several layers of tar paper, sealed with asphalt, then buried in soil to within 10 inches of its rim. Its plumbing and wiring—boxed in a wooden "tube"—run under deck 30 feet to support equipment adjoining house. Design: Ed Stiles.*

If you want to be bold

Spas and Tubs Create a Focal Point in the Garden

When you want to make a strong statement, you can let a hot tub or spa create a striking focal point in your landscape. First you site the hot bath where it will serve your needs best; then you structure a total environment around it, using plant material or decks.

If you have the space, you might consider the ultimate in strong statements—a separate structure for the hot bath, such as that shown on the facing page. (For Japanese-style structures, turn to pages 34–35.)

Narrow strip garden shown above runs width of back lot, is bounded by privacy wall and concrete patio. Owners wanted an outdoor hot bath but were reluctant to give up too much of the garden. The solution was an eye-catching, 5-foot-diameter wooden tub with compact-deck and stairs. Support equipment is behind metal gate at far right. Design: California Redwood Spa.

Tight space behind house became a total outdoor environment when spa was made focal point. Sunburst-pattern decking and steps emphasize its form. Design: Robert Clay.

Tudor-style garden gazebo, echoing stucco, brick, and wood construction of main house, is a quiet place to relax and rest. Also serving as a shelter for indoor plants, (see interior, below) the octagonal structure sits at the end of a small patio off home's den. French doors are opened for fresh air, closed for warmth. Design: California Redwood Spa.

Inside the gazebo, walls and benches are tongue-and-groove cedar, floor is redwood decking. Tidy look is achieved by lapping deck over top edge of tub, leaving enough space for snug-fitting cover (not shown), which rests flush with deck surface. Tub rests on a concrete slab, is surrounded by a concrete vault.

Garden Focal Point **47**

Redwood hot tub *(5 feet in diameter, 4 feet deep) takes advantage of a superb waterside view. Deck extends outdoor living space, and guests sometimes sail right up to join owners in a hot soak. Bench at right helps tubbers in and out of water; tub-level platform at left conceals support equipment.*

Expanding your outdoor living area

Two Hot Tubs That Take Advantage of a Special View

The views were already there. One took in rolling hills—green in spring, golden in autumn. The other was of open water—bright with sunshine during the day, sparkling with reflected lights at night.

So magnificent were the views that the homeowners insisted they be made a part of their new hot-tub installation. Working with designers, the owners achieved the best of two worlds: a hot bath that is close to the house and that takes advantage of the property's prime asset, the view.

Sweeping view *of valley and mountains is one of many bonuses of the hot-tub installation shown below. Originally a flat patio, tub area now includes a multilevel deck off master bedroom. Stone wall behind tub is both functional and esthetic: it gives privacy for soakers and baffles evening breezes; interior plumbing allows water to trickle down its face. Design: Nancy Benson.*

Fiberglass spa is used for hot soaking (especially during cooler months); long, narrow pool is used for lap swimming. Both employ a common heater/filter system, but spa has its own separate pump for hydro jets. When spa is in use, an automatic valve switches it off the pool system, allowing for higher water temperature in spa. Design: Galper and Baldon Associates.

First a swim, then a soak

They Wanted a Swimming Pool As Well As a Hot Bath

Here are two hot bath/swimming pool combinations that *work* in every sense of the word. One was designed as a unit; that is, the owners were ready for a swimming pool as well as a spa and wanted them to go in at the same time. Working closely with their designer, they gained pool, spa, and landscaping that are all part of a well-integrated scheme.

The other home already had a swimming pool, and the owners decided to add a hot bath—an addition, yes, but not an afterthought, for pool and hot bath work in perfect harmony.

This hot bath is actually a 5-foot fiberglass spa surrounded by redwood slats; "table" is center section of cover. Spa and redwood decking were added to an existing deck that surrounds the above-ground swimming pool seen in background. Solar panels on house roof and a heat exchanger attached to hot water heater raise temperature of spa when conditions permit. Spa and pool are not interconnected. Design: Gill Gillespie.

Seclusion, privacy,
and informality

Natural Hot Tubs in Natural Settings

Maybe it's a hot tub's unfinished wood that literally says "outdoors." Maybe it's the harmonious round form. Maybe it's the sparkling water. But, somehow, a tub seems *right* in a setting of trees, boulders, and other wild things.

As evidenced by the four varied installations shown on these two pages, a hot tub harmonizes with almost any natural setting. One rests in a thicket of aspens near a rushing creek; another fits into a rocky hillside; another tucks into a cluster of redwood trees; yet another nestles in a grove of oaks.

Countryside cedar hot tub is sited to take full advantage of a wooded setting. Tub rests in a below-grade insulated room, which protects it in freezing weather. Thermostat-controlled pump circulates water automatically if water temperature falls below 55° F/13° C. Design: Steve Moeller.

Hot tub family fun is in natural setting where privacy is no problem (installation is between house and rocky hillside). Like the massive rocks, redwood deck is at several levels, making benches unnecessary. Tub rests on concrete slab. Design: Marla Simpson.

Redwood grove *encloses redwood tub. Measuring 7 feet in diameter, 2½ feet deep, the shallow tub has no benches inside. Soakers sit on duckboard false floor that covers an air-bubbler ring. Resting on a concrete slab over chine joists, tub has, at rear, a shelf for seating or for towels. Heater, pump, and filter are located 40 feet away, near house.*

Freestanding *redwood tub (6 feet in diameter, 4 feet deep) is situated near property line under large oak tree. Towels hang on wooden pegs in fence; redwood rounds lead from tub to rear deck of house. Support equipment is located 30 feet away in a small shed.*

For that unused corner outdoors

Hot Tubs and Spas That Take Advantage of Little-used Space

Lost: Little-used space.
Gained: An extended area for outdoor living.

The three hot baths shown on these two pages have one thing in common: They are situated in an outdoor area that once was little used by their owners. Two of the spaces were relatively small, calling for a compact installation. The other space, being quite commodious (it was a roomy courtyard), was ideal for a large spa.

Tight space off master bedroom was seldom used by owners of hillside home until they installed a redwood hot tub. Bedroom wall and small fence (see plan) give soakers privacy and wind protection. Support equipment is located behind fence in enclosed cabinet insulated against freezing temperatures. Design: Colorado Hot Tub Co.

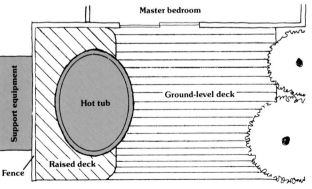

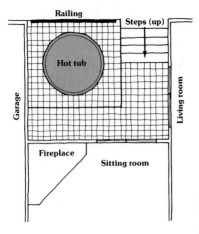

Cedar tub, 4 feet in diameter, 6 feet deep, fits snugly into small nook between living room, sitting room, and garage. Semicircular wooden lids form a kind of "headboard" for tub. Design: Paul Bickler, and Olympic Hot Tub Co.

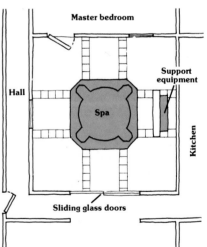

Enclosed courtyard originally had a tile fountain, which owners replaced with fiberglass spa. Spa is raised above grade approximately 1 foot by a cinderblock base backfilled with sand. Tile facing coordinates with house architecture. Design: Todd Fry.

Using Unused Space **53**

Adapting the greenhouse idea

Hot-tub Rooms That Bring the Outdoors Inside

Not all climates are suitable for year-round hot bathing outdoors. But the five installations shown on these two pages adapt the greenhouse idea to bring the sun's warmth inside. It's a way to control the environment immediately surrounding the hot-bath area. In addition, the spa and hot tub shown on the facing page are given a solar assist by double-glazed windows and by solar collectors that aid in heating the water for the hot bath.

Greenhouse-style tub room contains not just a hot tub (which rests on sleepers atop a concrete foundation), but also a sauna, a toilet, and an open shower. Skylight and glass doors keep room bright even on dark days. Design: Kenneth W. Nelson.

Cheery spa room with a view was gained when owners converted unused space below a cantilevered garage, making abundant use of glass in walls. Generous-sized spa (10 feet across) has four benches (each with its own hydro jet) and an air bubbler. Design: Lieb-Quaresma & Associates.

Two glass walls flood spa room with light and also give it a passive solar boost. Support equipment is housed in a below-deck concrete room. Design: Zaik, Miller, & Butler.

Cold-climate spa room is situated on south side of house, which receives the most year-round sun. Moist heat given off by spa makes an excellent environment for growing plants; wall louvers at base of double-glazed windows bring in fresh air. Spa is poured concrete faced with tile, and support equipment is housed under floor decking where it is protected from freezing. Design: Erdman & Lipsey.

Redwood hot tub "greenhouse" sits on concrete floor of former patio under a first-floor deck. Four 4 by 4-foot collector panels (shown in photograph at lower right) are used for heating domestic water supply; four other panels heat water for hot tub. Solar design: Solar Technology.

The Greenhouse Idea **55**

Dry heat/wet heat

Spa Plus Sauna Equal Home Health Center

Some people prefer wet heat. Some people prefer dry heat. Then there are those people who like both. The answer: A home health center that includes a spa (or hot tub) for simmering and a sauna for baking.

But doesn't all that equipment take a lot of room? Not as much as you might think. One of the installations shown on these two pages went together during construction of a new house. But the other two were conversions of existing space; one had been a basement workshop, the other a spare bedroom.

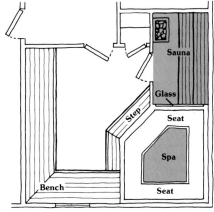

Home health center, containing spa, sauna, storage, and benches (see plan) was converted from a spare bedroom. Modest-sized 5 by 6-foot sauna seems more spacious because of its thermal window wall and door. Spa room has fan and two outside-opening windows to exhaust moisture-laden air. Spa support equipment is housed below benches. Design: David A. Konsmo.

Spa/sauna room, *converted from a former basement-level workshop, allows owners to bring the health club home. Floor of spa room (see far right) is covered with indoor-outdoor carpeting; walls and ceiling are paneled redwood sealed with clear urethane finish to resist moisture. Wood grating edges spa, covering drain that carries off splashed water. Sauna has two wider-than-average benches, one 24 inches above the floor, the other 44 inches. Design: David A. Konsmo.*

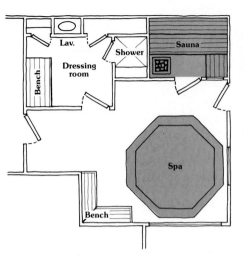

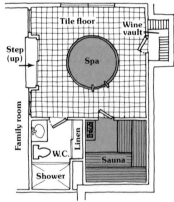

Spacious soaking room *(as viewed from sauna) has one window wall looking out on a deck. Below-floor-level redwood hot tub rests on redwood sills that are anchored to concrete blocks atop concrete slab sloped for drainage. This home health center has not only a bathroom and shower, but also a wine vault. Design: Glen A. Patterson.*

Home Health Center **57**

If you have space to spare . . .

Outdoor Saunas That Stand Alone

A freestanding outdoor sauna does require space. It also requires extra runs of plumbing and electrical wiring, or gas lines. But many sauna enthusiasts wouldn't have their sweat bath any other way.

"When I step out of the sauna I like to be outside, not inside," stated one owner.

Said another: "We had a swimming pool, so putting the sauna near it seemed like a good idea."

The sauna/swimming pool idea *is* a good one. Immediately after leaving the heated stove room you can plunge into cool water. Both of the sauna houses shown on pages 60–61 are situated adjacent to swimming pools.

Rustic freestanding sauna, attached to workshop off main house, has one door opening to forest, another leading to a dressing room and shower. Wood-burning brick stove (see below) has counterbalanced metal hood that is raised to lay the fire. Hood is then fitted snugly over firebox for heat buildup. Wood supply is kept just outside door.

Fire-stoking is done through cast-iron door in front of firebox, which also regulates draft. Stove has underground ash pit and a vent that draws fresh air from outside. Sauna house exterior is hand-split cedar shakes; interior paneling is 1 by 8-inch cedar. Concrete floor is covered with wooden duckboard. Design: Arch W. Diack.

Owner-built sauna has sturdy base of 4 by 4s resting on concrete patio between house and swimming pool. Plywood exterior, with decorative battens and cupola, is painted Wisconsin-barn style; roof is shingled. Interior paneling is 1 by 4-inch cedar. Floor space of approximately 40 square feet (height is 7 feet) accommodates six adults on two benches. Heater is 7.5-kilowatt electric unit. Design: James Dearborn.

...saunas that stand alone

Sturdy sauna house, looking like permanent part of forest, rests on concrete-pier foundation with retaining wall at backslope. Siding (1 by 6-inch boards, 1 by 2-inch battens) is untreated rough fir, which adds to natural appearance of structure. Asphalt shingles cover the roof. Windows bring light inside, yet are high enough for privacy. Situated near swimming pool, sauna house serves also as dressing room, as shown in plan below.

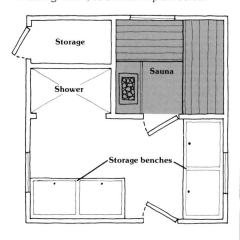

Stoveroom of sauna house shown above, measuring 6 by 9 feet (with 7-foot ceiling), is paneled in finished fir, has wood-burning stove. Benches are staggered to let three people stretch out, half a dozen sit. As shown in plan at far left, outer sauna room has a shower, benches for relaxing, and storage for towels, swimming pool accessories, and stove wood.

Custom-built sauna house—framed by backdrop of trees—rests on concrete foundation at one end of swimming pool. Siding is ⅝-inch resawn fir panels stained gray; roof is cedar shingles. Deck fronts the entire sauna house. See plan and interior view below.

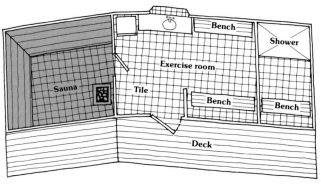

Stoveroom walls and ceiling are western red cedar; two-level benches are Alaskan yellow cedar. The 8 by 10-foot interior (with 7-foot ceiling) is heated by a 9-kilowatt electric stove. Ceramic tile on floor extends into exercise room. Instruments on far wall of stoveroom are sand timer and thermometer. Design: Finska Sauna.

Outdoor Saunas **61**

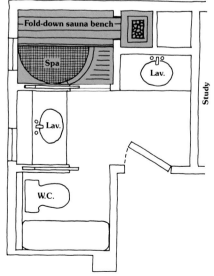

When space is at a premium

Squeezing In the Small-space Sauna

As hopeless as the small-space problem may sometimes seem, don't despair. The owners and designers of the saunas shown on these two pages did a remarkable job of finding a practical answer. One sauna was converted from an unused greenhouse (and in the process was given a solar boost by its double-glazed windows' being oriented to catch the sun's rays). Another was squeezed into an oddly shaped space (five sides!) behind a bathroom. Still another—perhaps the most unorthodox sauna of all—folds out of a wall to become a spa room.

Fold-out sauna bench in "down" position rests on rear half of circular spa (its rim is teak) in tiny room whose walls are half paneled with wood, half tiled. As shown in plan at right, 6-kilowatt electric heater is recessed into wall at end of bench. Reflective tiles around stove help heat room. Design: Douglas R. Zuberbuhler.

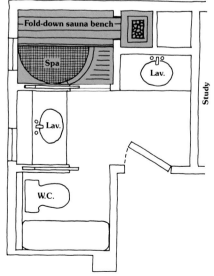

Once a greenhouse, *it's now a sauna, 8 by 8 feet, 7 feet high, and accessible from house kitchen through garage. Duckboards cover old greenhouse concrete floor. Electric sauna stove is rated at 8-kilowatts; unheated room temperature stays at 95° to 100° F/35° to 38° C because of solar heating of south-facing, double-glazed sky windows. Design: Reino Tarkiainen.*

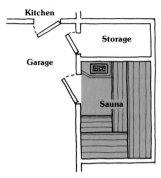

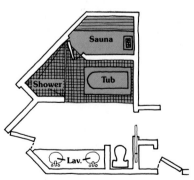

Cedar sauna— *only 4 by 7 feet—is squeezed into corner of bathroom behind hydro-jet tub, handy to shower. Heated by a 5-kilowatt electric stove, the room is just large enough for one bench, which accommodates one person lying down or two people sitting. Design: Morton Safford James III.*

Small Spaces **63**

A Room Full of Dry Heat

- **The sauna experience**
- **The modern sauna**
- **Sauna types**
- **Prefabricated saunas**
- **Anatomy of a sauna**
- **Sauna stoves**
- **Accessories**
- **Sauna care**

Known to Finns as the *sauna*, by as many other names as groups that practice it, dry-heat bathing is a 2,000-year-old custom that has warmed its way into the American scene with surprising speed since the late 1950s. Increasingly, Americans are discovering what Europeans have known all along—that the dry-heat bath is one of the most physically refreshing and mentally relaxing activities around.

Whether you're planning to build a sauna or buy one ready made, you'll benefit from the information in this sauna primer. Here you'll learn what to look for in sauna room construction, stoves, accessories, and custom touches. You'll find, too, help in planning the sauna's location, along with a little history, and instructions for taking the classic Finnish heat bath.

An early sauna — *from an 18th century etching by Giuseppe Acerbi.*

If you've never stretched out lazily on a bench in the heat of a 200°F/93°C room long enough to perspire freely from every pore in your body—and if you've never enjoyed the skintingling sensation of plunging into cool water (or a snowbank) afterward—you've missed the pleasure of a Finnish sauna.

Sauna (say "*sow*-na"—*sow* as in cow; "*saw*-na" if you prefer the American pronunciation) is the Finnish art of perspiration bathing. And, though the sweat bath has been with us for better than 2,000 years (the Greeks, Romans, Russians, Slavs, Turks, Africans, Germans, Eskimos, Irish, Mexicans, Mayans, and North American Indians all have practiced or still do practice it in one form or another), it is the Finns whom Americans have to thank for its growing popularity here.

The Sauna Experience

The sauna is an insulated wooden room heated from 160° to 200°F/71° to 93°C (sometimes even higher) that provides a restorative environment for the body. Its heat, usually very dry with less than 30 percent humidity, deep cleanses the skin through induced perspiration, stimulates circulation, and reduces muscular tension.

"Going to sauna" involves a cycle, repeated once or twice, that begins with a brief exposure to the intense heat of the wooden room, or stoveroom; gradual or rapid cooling with a shower, plunge into cool water, or—if you are a hardy sauna enthusiast—roll in the snow; and a period of quiet rest.

But the sauna experience is different for everyone because no two saunas are the same, and no two people respond to heat in the same way. You'll find as many variations on the sauna ritual—temperature of stoveroom, degree of humidity, length of stay, method of cooling, and so on—as you'll find sauna enthusiasts.

Health Benefits

"If spirits, tar, and the sauna can avail nothing, then there is no cure," goes an old Finnish saying, and even today some sauna enthusiasts are inclined to agree. The sauna has been attributed with healing everything from common colds to broken bones, although little medical research or evidence exists to support such claims.

Almost everyone agrees that the sauna makes you feel good. The combination of free perspiration, rapid cooling, and rest stimulates circulation to rid the body of impurities through the skin and liver, reduces muscular and nervous tension, and heightens mental awareness.

After strenuous workouts athletes often use the sauna to relax tired muscles. Some doctors prescribe it for patients with arthritis or rheumatism because the sauna's heat temporarily eases tension in the joints and muscles. It also has been known to temporarily relieve symptoms of colds, sinus congestion, and other minor respiratory ailments or allergies; poor circulation; tension headache; and acne (heat softens the oil plugs that block skin pores).

What the sauna does not do, as some diet faddists claim, is help you lose weight permanently. While it's true you'll weigh less after a sauna, the loss is primarily in water—very little fat is burned.

The Finnish Ritual

In Finland the sauna is as much a part of the culture as fast food stands are in America, though saunas undoubtedly are much better for you. In Finland there are more saunas than automobiles, and probably as

Birch whisk in hand, *a Finn crosses his snow-covered yard en route to the family sauna. The sauna is so deeply rooted in Finnish tradition that even war didn't interfere with its practice.*

many old sayings, such as "No Finn is without his sauna," or "Sauna makes a woman most beautiful one hour after the bath," or "Saturday sauna, milksoup, and girls." It was even common practice for a Finn to build his sauna before he built his house.

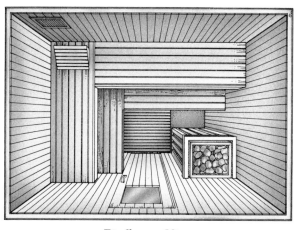

Bird's-eye View

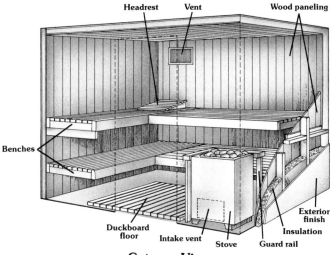

Headrest   Vent   Wood paneling

Benches

Duckboard floor   Intake vent   Stove   Guard rail   Insulation   Exterior finish

Cutaway View

The sauna is essentially a wood-paneled room, well insulated, ventilated, and heated by a specially designed stove. Two levels of benches, and perhaps a headrest or backrest, are its only furniture; bathers who like a "cooler" sauna stay on the lower level.

Not merely a source of physical renewal, the Finnish sauna is also regarded as a means of mental relaxation and quiet contemplation, as well as an activity to be shared by family and friends.

Saturday evening has customarily been reserved for the bath (though today any day of the week is suitable). After a good wood fire has heated stones in the sauna stove and warmed the walls and benches, family and perhaps a few neighbors gather for restful camaraderie in the soft heat of the "ripened" stoveroom. Children often sit on the lower benches, where it's cooler; adults usually prefer the hotter air higher up.

Within 5 or 10 minutes most bathers begin to perspire freely. Some leave the stoveroom to cool off in the fresh air, or in a nearby pond or stream, returning a few minutes later to the friendly heat of the sauna.

Bursts of invisible steam (*löyly*) punctuate the second visit to the stoveroom when one of the bathers ladles water over the hot stones to add moisture to the air. Then, taking *vihtas* (bundles of leafy birch twigs tied together) from their pegs, bathers whisk themselves lightly from head to toe, stimulating circulation and filling the air with a delicate birch fragrance.

A brisk scrubdown shower with soft brushes, perhaps another invigorating dip into cool water, and a time of relaxation over a *saunapala* —sauna snack—end the bath.

Sauna, American-style

Though the sauna arrived in America with the first Finnish immigrants in 1638, until the 1950s the heat bath was almost exclusively an ethnic practice. In fact, now and then the Finnish sauna aroused considerable suspicion among people who didn't understand how or why men, women, and children could or would sit naked together in a hot room and then jump around in the snow. Occasionally, innocent bathers walked out of the stoveroom into the hands of the law.

The high regard Finnish-Americans held for the sauna, however, gradually aroused the curiosity of other Americans who began to discover its invigorating benefits. Then, with the development of the electric sauna heater in Finland and Sweden in the 1930s, home saunas—easy to install and use—began to multiply.

By the 1960s sauna had become a household word, and sauna rooms began to appear in back yards, basements, apartment buildings, hotels, motels, resorts, sports locker rooms, and executive office suites.

The Modern Sauna Complex

"Sauna" is a Finnish word that technically refers to the room where the heat bath is taken, since for hundreds of years the entire sauna was simply a one-room cabin.

With an architectural metamorphosis from cabin to complex, however, "sauna" has come to refer to the triad of rooms—shower, dressing/relaxation, and stoveroom—as well as to the bathing process itself.

The Stoveroom: A One-Room Climate

Most important of the three rooms is the stoveroom, basically an insulated wooden box, usually rectangular, and simply furnished with two or three tiers of wooden benches. It is heated by a special stove designed to hold about 70 pounds (average for a family sauna) of igneous or metamorphic rocks (see "Stove Stones," page 77), which, when heated, pass a soft, pleasant heat into the room.

Properly designed and built, the stoveroom will provide just the right climate for an enjoyable heat bath. It should be well insulated, neither too big nor too small, correctly ventilated

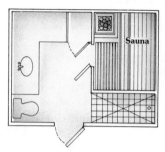

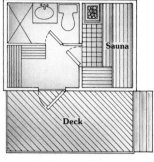

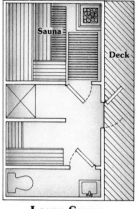

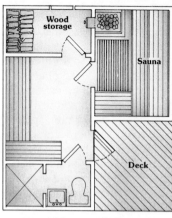

Small Indoor Sauna **Compact Sauna with Adjoining Deck** **Large Sauna with Adjoining Deck** **Wood-burning Sauna**

Contemporary saunas, whether linked to a bathroom or located outdoors, usually include dressing room and shower; some lead to open-air sitting spots.

and properly heated. Wood used for interior paneling and benches should stay pleasant to touch in a heated room, and benches should be wide enough to be comfortable for reclining bathers.

Design: size and shape. It's possible to have any shape or size sauna you want, but you should be aware of several rules of thumb that guide professional planners.

Size. Saunas range in size from tiny cubicles 3 by 3 by 7′ high for prefabricated mini-saunas that squeeze into closets and other small spots, to roomy 12 by 16 by 9′ high for public saunas that accommodate large numbers of bathers.

The size sauna you choose should depend on 1) the number of people you expect to be using the sauna at once (allow 65 cubic feet, about 2.5 cubic yards, of space for each bather); 2) the amount of space available for the stoveroom, and perhaps accompanying dressing room and bath; 3) arrangement of the benches (one wall dimension should be at least 6 feet long so you can lie down); 4) the size stove your budget can afford; and 5) your over-all budget. Two popular sizes for family saunas are 5 by 7 by 7′ high, or 6 by 6 by 7′ high; larger rooms generally require more powerful and thus more expensive stoves, extra lumber for framing, paneling, and benches, and additional batts of insulation.

Regardless of the floor dimen-

sions, standard recommended ceiling height is 7 feet for family saunas. This lower-than-average ceiling prevents heat from rising into unused space.

Shape. By far the most popular shapes, rectangles and square saunas allow for maximum use of bench space—an important consideration in sauna use. Octagonal, round, even wedge-shaped saunas aren't unknown, but you cannot expect their bench arrangements to offer the same flexibility.

Dressing Room and Shower

For the simple reason that the sauna involves a heating-cooling-rest process, most saunas are installed near or designed to include a dressing room and shower.

The dressing room, often the same size or larger than the stoveroom, is usually furnished with benches, a closet or pegs for clothing, a small linen closet for extra towels and accessories, and a place to put jewelry, watches, and glasses.

If your dressing room is the only place you have to cool off (and it's often the case with freestanding saunas), plan for wide benches, perhaps cushioned, so you can stretch out comfortably.

Locating Your Sauna

Few people are fortunate enough to have wooded property that opens to a placid pond or bubbling stream—

the classic setting for traditional Finnish saunas. If you number among the few, there's probably no question where your sauna will go (unless building codes restrict you).

Fortunately, it's not necessary to have a picturesque setting for your sauna. You are still free to enjoy its invigorating benefits whether you put the stoveroom outdoors or in, near a swimming pool, or in a corner of the basement.

Outdoor saunas. Outdoors may be a particularly good location for your sauna if you can install it near an existing swimming pool; this way, you're only a few steps away from a plunge into cool water after you leave the stoveroom.

You also may prefer an outdoor sauna if you can tuck it into an unused corner of the yard that's made private with trees and shrubs. Include outdoor furniture or benches in your plan so you can relax in the open air between stoveroom visits.

Your primary consideration in erecting an outdoor sauna is the cost of plumbing, electric wiring (220-volt as well as 110-volt), or gas lines (if gas is your source of heat).

When you do install an outdoor sauna, try to situate it on level ground, and—to avoid offending neighbors—plan on privacy screens or hedges if you like post-stoveroom plunges into your pool in your birthday suit.

Indoor saunas. Indoors you have many options for a stoveroom location, as well as the advantage of

having the sauna close by on wet winter days.

If the sauna is adjacent to the master bath, you also often have all the advantages of an existing dressing room, shower, and rest area.

Or, consider converting part of your utility room, an extra storeroom or pantry, or a basement corner into a sauna. Also consider attic space, a spare bedroom, or part of your garage. In most cases existing walls and floor can be used to simplify the stoveroom construction.

Your Options in Saunas

Today the home sauna buyer has a wealth of options in sauna design, construction, and materials that suit almost any taste and budget.

Prefabricated, or modular, saunas —kits that come complete with framed, insulated, and paneled walls

Assembling a Prefab Sauna

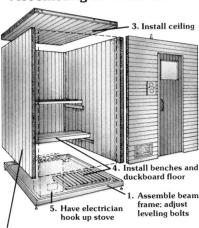

3. Install ceiling

4. Install benches and duckboard floor

1. Assemble beam frame; adjust leveling bolts

5. Have electrician hook up stove

2. Bolt, snap, or lock wall panels to frame according to manufacturer's instructions

and ceiling, benches, door, sauna stove, and hardware—are so streamlined that it's possible to snap, bolt, or lock one together in the space of an afternoon.

You can buy a sauna kit for almost any size room indoors; and, if you want your sauna outdoors, you can purchase a kit that includes exterior roof and siding. Some manufacturers even sell sauna complexes or cottages that include dressing room,

shower, and sometimes even a kitchenette and small bedroom.

Most manufacturers are willing to make some custom modifications for prefabricated rooms, such as building wider benches or providing a different exterior finish.

Precut saunas also are available; using your specifications many sauna manufacturers will provide a bundle of materials (interior paneling, framing lumber, insulation batts, stove, etc.) for you to assemble. Precut saunas might be your best bet if you're handy with a hammer.

Custom-built saunas suit oddly shaped spaces and more sophisticated tastes, and usually are designed by architects or sauna builders. They offer the greatest design flexibility, but they are often more expensive than prefabricated or precut units. A custom sauna can be as traditional as a Finnish log house situated by a stream, as unorthodox as a shower stall that doubles as a stoveroom.

If you plan to build your sauna from scratch, you can purchase almost any of the materials, including stove, control panel, and hardware, from a sauna manufacturer or retail distributor.

How to Buy a Prefab Sauna

Shopping for a prefabricated (or modular) sauna is very similar to shopping for a major household appliance or automobile—you need to do a little research before you make your decision.

You'll find only about a dozen manufacturers of prefabricated saunas in the United States. Some are large, with distributors in most metropolitan areas; others are small, one or two-person operations with sales restricted to a single region. All sell standard packages, either for indoor or outdoor installation, and a few also manufacture custom modular units to suit an architect's specifications or your own needs.

Whether standard or custom-built, prefabricated saunas usually come in easy-to-handle packages with

parts numbered to coincide with step-by-step assembly instructions. The only tools you usually need to assemble one are a hammer, screwdriver, framing square and level, and perhaps a drill.

Before you choose a prefabricated sauna, read about sauna construction in the following section, "Anatomy of a Well-built Sauna." Whether a sauna is custom-built or prefabricated, certain standards exist for materials used in construction as well as for construction techniques. Knowing them will help you when you compare prefabricated units for quality of design, materials, and workmanship.

Next, visit dealers in your area, examine their display models, and ask for literature, price lists, and a copy of assembly instructions. (Don't be dazzled by slick promotional literature; some manufacturers of fine quality saunas and stoves will have only mimeographed or photocopied brochures to give you.)

Then, as you compare saunas, examine their design, materials used in construction, ease of installation, dealer warranty, and package weight. Compare the packages as well; some manufacturers include everything but the floor; others may also exclude exterior finishes, stove, or stove controls, depending on their pricing systems. (In some cases you may want to purchase the room from one manufacturer and the correct size stove from another.)

You also may find it worth your time to ask your sauna distributor to show you several saunas that have been installed longer than a year. Talk to homeowners to find out if they are satisfied with their sauna's construction as well as performance of the stove and sauna controls.

Anatomy of a Well-built Sauna

Whether you plan to build your own sauna or buy a prefabricated or precut unit, the following information

will help you understand what's important and peculiar to sauna construction, from foundation to finishing touches.

Consider a sauna addition as you would the addition of a room to your house. Like a room addition, a sauna requires an adequate foundation, proper flooring, framing, wiring, insulation, interior and exterior finishes, and furniture and decorative details that make the sauna functional and comfortable.

If you are an experienced home craftsman you probably can build your own sauna over a period of several weekends. If not, give the job to a reliable sauna builder, or a contractor with sauna-building experience; perhaps you can make arrangements to do some of the minor tasks yourself. Usually it's not difficult installing insulation, for instance, and if you don't mind a little backbreaking labor, you probably can dig foundation trenches.

If you choose to have your sauna built by a sauna specialist or contractor, do some preliminary checking. Ask to see several saunas installed by the contractor and talk to the people who own them. Base your final choice on the builder's reputation rather than on the lowest bid; he should be well-established, licensed, cooperative, financially solvent, and insured for workmen's compensation, property damage, and public liability.

If you decide to build your own sauna, you'll find helpful construction information in other *Sunset* building books listed on the back cover; in *The International Handbook of Finnish Sauna* by Allan Konya and Alewyn Burger (New York: Halsted Press, 1973); and *The Sauna Book* by Tom Johnson and Tim Miller (New York: Harper & Row, 1977).

For general background information on the Finnish sauna you also may enjoy reading John O. Virtanen's *The Finnish Sauna* (Portland, Ore.: Continental Publishing, 1974) and H. J. Viherjuuri's *Sauna: The Finnish Bath* (Brattleboro, Vt.: The Stephen Greene Press, 1965).

Heat bathing in different cultures is described by Mikkel Aaland in *Sweat* (Santa Barbara: Capra Press, 1978).

Foundations and Floors

The type of foundation and floor your sauna needs depends on where it's located, what kind of floor surface you prefer, your climate, and the condition and slope of your property if the sauna is to be freestanding (or attached to the existing structure).

Foundations. Indoors, where you are converting existing space into a sauna, all you may need to do initially is to put down a wood frame and subfloor over the existing floor; the

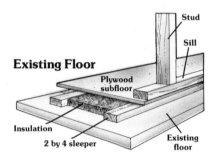

Existing Floor

Stud, Sill, Plywood subfloor, Insulation, 2 by 4 sleeper, Existing floor

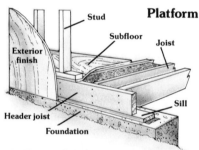

Platform

Stud, Subfloor, Joist, Exterior finish, Header joist, Foundation, Sill

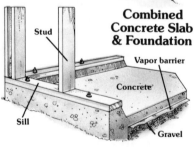

Combined Concrete Slab & Foundation

Stud, Vapor barrier, Concrete, Sill, Gravel

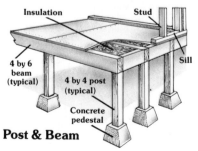

Post & Beam

Insulation, Stud, Sill, 4 by 6 beam (typical), 4 by 4 post (typical), Concrete pedestal

Three Floor Finishes

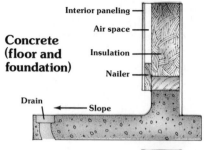

Concrete (floor and foundation)

Interior paneling, Air space, Insulation, Nailer, Drain, Slope

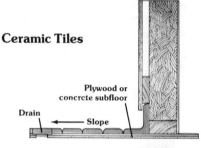

Ceramic Tiles

Plywood or concrete subfloor, Drain, Slope

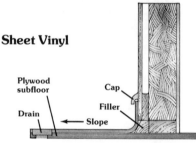

Sheet Vinyl

Plywood subfloor, Cap, Filler, Drain, Slope

existing floor serves as the foundation.

If you are building an outdoor sauna and you live in an area where the ground doesn't freeze, you can install foundation and floor at the same time by putting down a slab of concrete over sand or fine gravel (see illustrations above and left) that's covered with a sheet of heavy polyethylene plastic. The plastic keeps moisture from penetrating the concrete.

Where the ground does freeze, you must install a more substantial foundation of wood or masonry construction, below frost line, which will resist damage caused by frost heaving. You may also want to insulate the floor; if the foundation is of wood construction you can place rock wool or fiberglass batts between the floor joists.

Floors. The floor is the coolest spot (80° to 100°F/27° to 38°C) in a heated sauna, so you can use almost anything from concrete to tile as a surfacing material.

The best sauna floors are waterproof and slightly sloped toward drains so that water can be used in the sauna during the heat bath and for cleaning. (Water permitted to leak through flooring will eventually cause mildew or dry rot in the wood structure beneath.)

Wooden duckboards (racks of wood strips with spaces between) are often used over concrete floors because they're simple to install, attractive, and easily removed when the sauna needs cleaning. Over a concrete slab, you also can use plastic slats made for sauna use, or woven matting that can be removed for periodic cleaning; or you can surface the floor with ceramic tiles.

Duckboard Construction

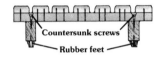

Countersunk screws
Rubber feet

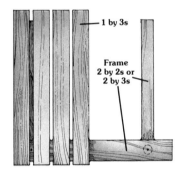

1 by 3s

Frame 2 by 2s or 2 by 3s

For a waterproof floor over a plywood base, you can use ceramic tile, seamless sheet vinyl, or fiberglass. Slope the floor toward a drain, and use only waterproof adhesives during installation.

Though they aren't waterproof, solid wood floors are nonetheless a traditional surfacing material for saunas. Wood is a good insulator and esthetically pleasing, but it also becomes slippery when wet, quickly absorbs perspiration odors, and can be difficult to clean properly. (You should limit the amount of water used in a sauna with a solid wood floor to protect the foundation from dry rot.)

Indoor-outdoor carpeting is installed in a number of prefabricated saunas, though some sauna experts feel that there is a tendency to trap and breed bacteria.

Framing, Wiring, and Insulation

With your foundation laid you are ready to frame the floor (unless your foundation is a concrete slab), walls, and ceiling; then to wire and insulate.

Framing. If you've poured a slab foundation that will serve as the sauna floor you can begin framing the walls. If not, you first must construct a subfloor over floor joists that are nailed to the sill plate (see illustration below).

When framing the walls, perhaps the easiest technique is to assemble studs, sills, plates, and headers for the door and windows, one section at a time, directly on the slab or subfloor. Each wall section, once assembled, is erected, squared, and nailed to the floor joists through the subfloor, or attached to the concrete slab with anchor bolts or concrete nails.

Rafters, like joists and studs, should be spaced according to code requirement, usually 16″ or 24″ on center.

Wiring. Unless you are an experienced electrician, hire a professional to install the electrical circuits for 1) your stove, control panel, and thermostat, and 2) the lighting. Elec-trical standards are strict and precise; in a sauna you usually must use wiring than can hold up under 194°F/90°C or higher temperatures, and that will withstand moist conditions. You also must locate the wires in dry areas behind the insulation. Check first with your building inspector.

A typical sauna wiring scheme is illustrated on page 71. Note that all switches must go on the outside of the stoveroom.

Insulation. Good insulation in a sauna keeps heat in and the cost of operating your stove down.

Your best choice is one of two types of mineral wool: fiberglass, made from glass fiber; and rock wool, spun from molten slag rock. These insulation materials come in flexible blankets and batts (fiberglass also comes in rigid boards), and they're usually easy for an amateur home craftsman to handle. (Always wear gloves, long-sleeved shirts, loose clothing, and safety glasses when installing mineral wool, though. Stray fibers can sorely irritate the skin.)

When selecting insulation, consider the material's "R" rating rather than its thickness. The R value tells you a material's ability to stop the flow of heat—the higher the rating, the more effective the material.

Framing and Insulation

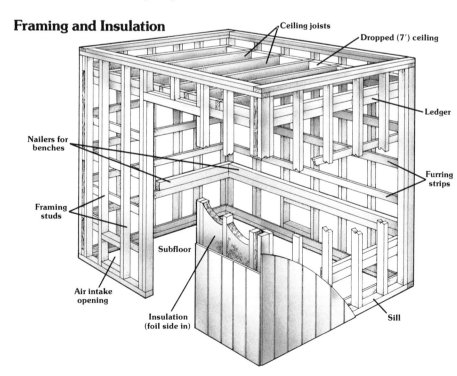

Ceiling joists
Dropped (7′) ceiling
Ledger
Nailers for benches
Furring strips
Framing studs
Subfloor
Air intake opening
Insulation (foil side in)
Sill

Wiring the Sauna

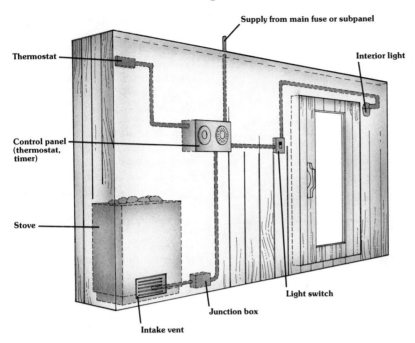

Supply from main fuse or subpanel

Thermostat

Interior light

Control panel (thermostat, timer)

Stove

Light switch

Junction box

Intake vent

Since R value requirements vary from region to region (along the West Coast, for example, an exterior wall requires insulation with an R-value of 11; along the East Coast an exterior wall requires R-19 insulation). Check with your building department for R-value requirements in your area.

A frequent choice for sauna insulations is foil-faced fiberglass (3½-inch-thick batts usually have an R value of 11). The batts come in 15″ and 23″ widths with flanges you can staple (do not use glue) to framing studs. The foil side should face in: it creates a vapor barrier to prevent moisture from collecting inside the walls, and it reflects some heat back into the sauna.

Doors and Windows

Like the rest of sauna construction, doors and windows must be built to contribute to the sauna's specialized climate. Both must be insulated and properly fitted to the jamb or frame to minimize heat loss.

Doors. When you hang your sauna door it's important to keep in mind that it will shrink and swell with

changes in temperature. If your door doesn't fit just right into the jamb, you may end up either fighting to open it or fighting to keep heat from slipping through the cracks.

Sauna doors measure 6′ to 6′8″ high by 20″ or 24″ wide (the smaller size is better in a small sauna, where heat loss is particularly high every time you open the door). For safety reasons, sauna doors should always open out; they should never be fitted with latching devices that can malfunction and lock you in.

You can either buy prehung doors made specifically for saunas from sauna manufacturers, or you can make your own from a standard solid core door purchased from a supplier that handles custom sizes. (Don't try to build a 6-foot sauna door from a standard 6′8″ solid core door; cutting 8 inches from it to suit the sauna will expose the core to moisture and

eventually give you a warped door.) When you do use a solid core door you need to add a frame (see illustration below), insulation, and paneling.

Sauna doors generally require three hinges (4″ brass butt or spring-loaded) to carry their weight, ball or roller catches (never any that can lock you in), and wood handles.

Windows. Even the smallest window will eliminate the claustrophobic feeling you can get in a stoveroom. Windows, too, let daylight into the room and can give you visual access to a pleasant view.

Whether it's a small square in a door or an entire window wall, your window should be made of thermal glass—double-glazed or double pane tempered glass (or plexiglass) with air space between. It should be hermetically sealed to prevent moisture from collecting inside the panes.

When you install the glass, make an allowance for it to swell slightly in the heat. If it fits too tightly in the frame, the glass is likely to crack when it expands. Also avoid using metal frames or hardware that will become too hot to touch.

Interior Paneling

Interior walls in classic Finnish saunas were simply the other side of exterior walls—rough, adzed logs harvested from spruce and pine forests. The logs were dotted with knotholes, and resins yielded a faint woody smell in the heated stoveroom. The hot knotholes and melting resins also sometimes burned bathers.

Interior walls and ceilings in today's custom-built and prefabricated saunas are usually surfaced

The Sauna Door

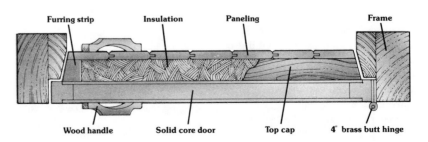

Furring strip **Insulation** **Paneling** **Frame**

Wood handle **Solid core door** **Top cap** **4″ brass butt hinge**

Paneling the Sauna

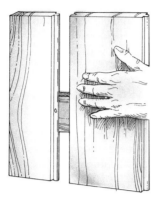

1. Slide groove of panel over tongue

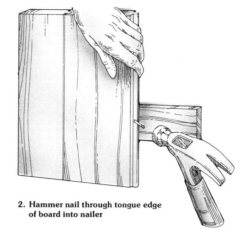

2. Hammer nail through tongue edge of board into nailer

with unblemished, high grade woods that are kiln-dried to resist shrinking, cupping, and warping. They are also milled smooth for comfort.

You should avoid finishing the walls and ceiling with any nonwood materials, such as tile, vinyl, fabric, or metals; these materials can become toxic or too hot to touch, or they can constitute a fire hazard. (Using stone, tile, or brick as a fireproof surface near the stove is one exception to this rule.)

Choosing wood. The best woods to use for interior paneling are low-density softwoods which resist heat (dense woods absorb it) and thus remain comfortable to touch in a heated stoveroom. Such woods include redwood, western red cedar, Alaskan yellow cedar, eastern white pine, and sugar pine. Also included are ponderosa pine, spruce, and hemlock, as well as the somewhat denser cypress and Douglas fir. (Cedar is particularly known for its distinctive aroma, which minimizes perspiration odors.)

You can purchase paneling either from a sauna distributor who sells precut lumber or from your local lumber dealer. Choose finished, vertical grain woods (flat-grained woods tend to splinter) that are relatively free of knotholes and exposed resin pockets; boards that have these flaws should be located near the floor (never on the ceiling), away from bathers. Try to use continuous lengths of wood for paneling to minimize joints that can trap moisture and dirt.

Installation. One way to install interior paneling (sauna builders often use 1 by 4 or 1 by 6 V-grooved tongue and groove boards) is to blind nail it vertically to the framing studs. Using rust-resistant, hot-dipped galvanized finish nails or staples, nail (or staple) through the tongue edge of each board (see illustration above) so the groove of the next panel will hide the nails.

With either tongue and groove or shiplap boards, or their variations, you also can panel horizontally or diagonally, or use a wood pattern of your own design.

Exterior Finishes

Any number of materials—wood shakes or shingles, aluminum, wood, or plywood siding, wallboard, face brick, or stone veneer—may be used for the sauna exterior. Your choice will ultimately be determined by your sauna's location, your personal taste and budget, and local building requirements.

The sauna exterior should blend with the architectural style of your house and landscape if the sauna is outdoors; if indoors, it should have an exterior finish that complements the room interiors.

If you use lumber you can paint, varnish or seal it, though it's a good idea to choose a finish that doesn't require frequent reapplication. If the sauna is outdoors, you may prefer to finish it with wood that weathers naturally.

Benches

Sauna furnishings are usually wooden platforms that permit bathers to sit or stretch out comfortably. But, because bathers' skin comes into direct contact with the bench, wood used in bench construction must be chosen with care.

Woods to use. Clear heartwoods of white pine, poplar, or cedar are often used for sauna benches because they remain comfortable to touch in a heated stoveroom, resist splintering, and have no knotholes or pitch pockets that can cause burns.

Design. Most family saunas have two levels of benches (18″ to 30″ wide, and sometimes wider) arranged in an L-shape in order to fully utilize stoveroom space. In larger saunas the benches may be arranged in tiered rows along one wall, or in U-shaped configurations as well. Other saunas have two or three small steps that lead to a single, gallerylike platform.

When you have two levels of benches, the lower one should be about 18″ from the floor (average chair height), and the uppermost about 42″ from the ceiling to allow seated bathers adequate head space.

Typical bench configurations are shown on page 73.

Construction. The best benches are slatted because they encourage air circulation, prevent perspiration from accumulating, and allow for easy cleaning. They may be built of 2 by 2s, 2 by 3s, or 2 by 4s, and should be spaced no more than ½ inch apart (see illustration, page 74). Nails should be either counter-sunk and filled, or hammered through the underside bracing to keep nailheads away from bathers.

Installation. If your sauna walls are sturdy enough, you can support the benches with 2 by 4s attached to the walls (see illustration, page 74). Or you can support the benches partly by the walls and partly by the floor, or with wooden legs. If the benches are free-standing, it's a good idea to install leveling bolts that allow for adjustments and raise the legs just off the floor so their ends cannot absorb moisture.

Bench Patterns

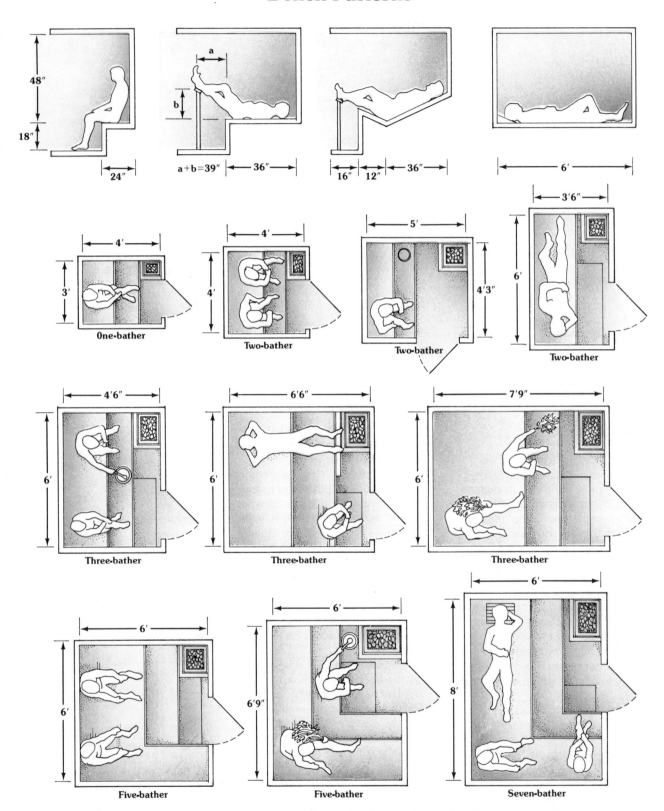

Both small saunas and spacious ones *are most functional when benches are designed to allow bathers to sit or stretch out comfortably at one or more levels in the room. Lower benches are generally flat surfaces, but upper benches can be curved or angled to suit individual preferences. In both mini- and larger saunas, the most practical and flexible bench arrangements are L-shaped and parallel. (Adapted, with permission, from* The International Handbook of Finnish Saunas *by Allan Konya and Alewyn Burger, New York: John Wiley & Sons, 1973.)*

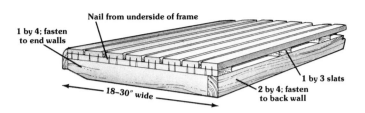

Nail from underside of frame

1 by 4; fasten to end walls

1 by 3 slats

18–30" wide

2 by 4; fasten to back wall

Typical Bench Construction

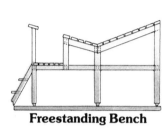

Freestanding Bench

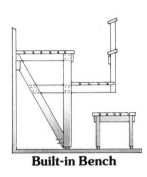

Built-in Bench

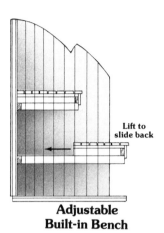

Lift to slide back

Adjustable Built-in Bench

Sauna benches are usually tiered to allow bathers their choice of levels, and therefore of temperature (the higher, the hotter). If the room has enough space, foot rests can be built—as in the freestanding and built-in models shown above—enabling bathers to stretch out in complete comfort.

Lighting

Subdued lighting, whether from natural sources or electrical fixtures, is usually most appealing in a sauna. Strong, bright lights detract from the relaxing spirit of the sauna and can create an unpleasant glare.

Light fixtures generally are located high on a wall away from the stove, or sometimes in recessed fixtures in the ceiling. Since switches aren't made to stand up under high heat or moist conditions, they always should be located outside the sauna.

You can buy vapor-sealed fixtures designed to prevent moisture from coming in contact with the bulb and socket.

Unless you are a skilled electrician, let a professional wire for lighting.

Ventilation

Proper ventilation is important to sauna design and construction: it provides a continuous, free flow of

air in the room, oxygen for bathers, and a means of escape for stale air; it also allows the stove to draw fresh air up through the hot stones.

It's especially important to provide adequate ventilation in saunas with gas- and wood-burning stoves, since wood fires draw oxygen from the air supply in the room. Bathers in a poorly vented sauna can become dizzy or even asphyxiated. Your building department can tell you how much vent area is required for your sauna—usually 1/20 the floor area but not less than 1½ square feet.

The intake vent should be located near the floor, in the wall behind the stove (some are installed in the sauna door); for proper cross-ventilation place the outlet on the opposite wall, approximately level with (not below) the intake vent, or a few inches from the ceiling. The outlet should have an adjustable slide cover that allows you to control the amount of air leaving the room. If the outlet leads directly outside, provide an up-draft duct to avoid back pressure that can draw additional cool air into the sauna.

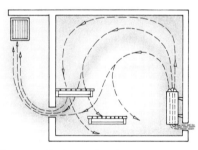

Air circulation with exhaust vent placed low on wall opposite air intake.

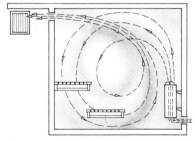

Air circulation with exhaust vent placed high on wall opposite air intake.

Building Codes and Zoning Laws

Before you build your sauna, check with your city or county building department to learn which regulations affect your sauna's design, location, or construction.

Building codes. Exasperating though they may be, building codes set minimum requirements for structural design and construction materials, ensuring that buildings are sound and durable.

Codes vary according to community, but most set similar standards based on the Uniform Building Code (UBC) and National Electrical Code (NEC) for foundations, framing, and wiring. In the case of saunas, some may specify a certain type of insulation for the stoveroom.

Zoning laws. Basically, zoning laws regulate community land use, dividing it into residential, commercial, and industrial sectors. But they also set some restrictions on property use, such as maximum building height, minimum distances between structures and property lines, and the amount of lot structures may cover.

Variances. If plans for your sauna project violate zoning ordinances, you can apply for a variance through your building department. Minor deviations may be given an "administrative variance," but major ones usually require approval by an appointed board of appeal.

Building permits. Check with your building department to find out which permits you need to build your sauna.

Sauna Stoves

A good stove is the heart of the sauna. One that's properly designed and the right size for the room will provide the soft, pleasant heat characteristic of the finest Finnish heat baths.

The simplest of all sauna stoves was a wood fire beneath a pile of stones. These stoves, occasionally still in use in the classic *savusaunas* (smoke saunas) in rural Finland, had no chimneys. When the fire had heated the stones and its smoke had slowly filtered out of the sauna through small vents near the ceiling or floor (sometimes it took up to 20 hours!) the sauna was considered "ripened" and ready for use.

Modern prefabricated stoves— gas, electric, and wood—all are modeled after the simple savusauna stove (though wood-heated stoves now have chimneys to vent the smoke). Fuel heats the stones, which heat the room—often in less than an hour.

How to Choose a Stove

To determine which type of stove your sauna should have—gas, electric, or wood-burning—weigh the cost of installation with the monthly cost of operation.

If, for example, electricity is your most economical source of fuel, you may opt for an electric stove. But if it's going to cost you an additional $500 to $1,000 to run a 220-volt supply to the sauna, you may be better off with a gas stove that costs only $300 to install, even if it costs a little more per month to operate.

If you plan to use a wood-heating stove, you should be near a good supply of the kind of wood that burns well in a sauna (see page 77 for further information).

Other things to consider when you buy a prefabricated stove:
• Will it fit through the door of your sauna?
• Is it powerful enough to heat the stoveroom to the desired temperature?
• How much time does it take (35-45 minutes is desirable) to heat the sauna?
• Can it make the stones hot enough to produce steam when you pour water over them?
• Does the stove carry an adequate supply of stones?
• If the heater fails, can it be repaired locally?
• What guarantee does the manufacturer offer?
• If electric, does it meet UL (Underwriters Laboratories) standards for wiring? If gas, does it meet AGA (American Gas Association) standards?
• Is it constructed to handle extremes in heat and humidity over a long period of time?
• How much will it cost to run gas pipes or a 220-volt service to the room?
• Do you need to install a higher capacity electrical service?

Safety measures. If yours is an approved Underwriters Laboratories (UL) or American Gas Association (AGA) stove, it's usually not necessary to locate it near fireproof walls and floor. It is important, however, to allow the proper wall-to-stove clearance suggested by manufacturers (4 to 10 inches). Wood-burning stoves may be installed adjacent to a brick or stone wall for additional fire protection.

To protect bathers from the stove, install a wood railing or fence around it.

Electric stoves. Electric stoves are by far the most popular choice of sauna heater because they are clean, efficient, easy to install, and economical (unless you live in an area where electricity is costly). Electric elements, similar to those in a kitchen stove but designed specifically for sauna use, heat a pile of stones (up to 60 kilos, or 132 pounds) that are placed either in a metal tray over the elements, or directly among them (see illustration, page 76).

The elements are usually encased in one or two, sometimes even three, layers of noncorrosive metal with air between. The outermost casing, usually of stainless steel or baked enamel, helps to keep the surface from becoming too hot and discourages heat loss from the sides and front of the unit.

Electric stoves come in both wall-mounted and freestanding models, though the freestanding type are often more desirable because they can carry up to twice the weight in

Electric Sauna Stoves

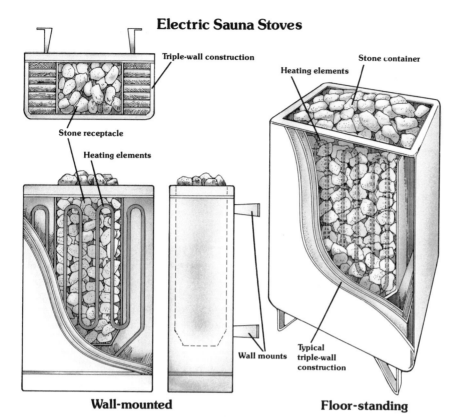

Wall-mounted

Floor-standing

stoveroom volume (V=room length x width x height) by 45 to know how many kilowatts are needed in the stove ($\frac{V}{45}$=kw). For a sauna that measures 5 by 7 by 7,' with a volume of 245 cubic feet, a 5.5 or 6 kw stove should provide adequate heat.

Gas Stoves

Gas stoves, because of their flues, are a little more complicated but usually less expensive to install and less expensive to operate than electric stoves, and they are far more efficient in their use of fuel.

Like electric stoves, gas stoves are metal-encased, thermostatically controlled, and equipped with a safety device that shuts off the gas if the pilot light is extinguished.

When the stove is operating, gas is fed at a constant pressure to a small burner in a sealed combustion chamber (see illustration below) below the pile of stones. Air is drawn into the chamber from outside the sauna and expelled through the flue.

If you choose a gas stove you'll need to run gas lines to its location, or install tanks of liquid propane outside.

What size gas stove? Gas stoves are sized according to the amount of heat, measured in British Thermal Units (BTUs), the heater generates.

Gas-heated Stove

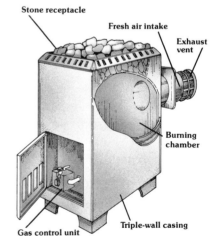

stones of wall-mounted units. Where space is at a premium, wall-mounted units may be the most suitable.

A control panel located just outside the stoveroom (controls should never go inside the stoveroom—they aren't constructed to withstand high temperatures and can become too hot to touch) includes a thermostat that regulates temperature, a switch for the stove, a small red signal light, and sometimes a 60-minute timer or 24-hour automatic timer. The stove itself is equipped with a high-limit safety device that cuts off the electrical current in event of a malfunction.

If you choose an electric stove for your sauna, you'll need to hook it up to a 220-volt supply (the same voltage that operates your kitchen range and clothes dryer). Some of the smallest electric stoves plug into 110-volt outlets, but they can be costly to operate and ineffective in anything but mini-saunas designed to accommodate one or two bathers.

When you install a 220-volt stove, check with your electric company or building department to learn what your electrical requirements are. In many cases your electrician can run wiring from the stove to the main

fuse box, or to a subpanel near the sauna. In some cases, however, especially when a home power supply cannot support the additional demands of a sauna stove, you'll need to install a new electrical service.

What size electric stove? Having the right size stove in your sauna is important; a stove that's too powerful for the room will heat it too quickly for the stones to do their work, and a stove that's too small will never get the room, or the stones, as hot as you want them.

Electric stoves are measured by the number of kilowatts (1kw=1000 watts) used to heat the elements; they are available in 2.2 to 18kw models.

Choosing the right size electric stove depends both on the size sauna you want to heat, and on the sauna's location (and climate if it is outdoors). A 5 by 7 by 7' sauna located outdoors in the path of prevailing winter winds, for example, requires a more powerful stove than the same size sauna situated indoors with no walls exposed to cold weather.

As a general rule of thumb in a temperate climate, however, allow 1 kw for every 45 cubic feet of room space. To compute stove size, divide

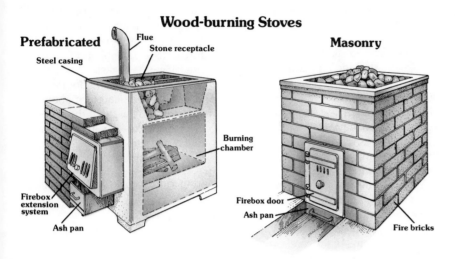

Wood-burning Stoves

Prefabricated

Steel casing

Flue

Stone receptacle

Firebox extension system

Ash pan

Burning chamber

Masonry

Firebox door

Ash pan

Fire bricks

As with electric stoves, the size gas stove your sauna requires depends on the size stoveroom, its location, and climate. Generally you should allow 1,000 BTUs for every 15 cubic feet of stoveroom volume. (A 5 by 7 by 7′ stoveroom with a volume of 245 cubic feet will require a 16,000 BTU gas heater.)

Wood Stoves

If wood is an abundant source of fuel in your area, you may want a wood-burning stove. Enthusiasts who have wood stoves almost without exception regard the wood-heated sauna as the ultimate in Finnish heat bathing. (They also are inclined to point out that wood-heated saunas have a 2,000-year head start on the others.)

It is the quality of the heat that is so highly regarded by sauna connoisseurs; and, although it takes longer for a wood stove to heat a sauna, the appealing scent of the wood that penetrates the walls cannot be matched in an electric or gas-heated room.

With the exception of the flue and chimney, which allows the smoke to escape outside the stoveroom, the wood stove is by design identical to the classic smoke sauna stove: a fire box below a pile of stones, often built of bricks or river stones.

Several sauna manufacturers sell prefabricated wood-burning stoves, constructed of corrosive-resistant metal; some are equipped with extension systems so the fire can be stoked outside the stoveroom.

Though the romance of the wood-burning stove cannot be denied, these stoves do have disadvantages. It can take a long time—2 to 4 hours—for a wood fire in a masonry unit to ripen a stoveroom (manufactured stoves are usually more efficient), and every fire leaves ashes which you must remove periodically. You must decide, too, who is going to chop all that wood—about 20 kilos (44 pounds) of good, dense wood are required to heat an average-size family sauna.

Wood as fuel. The type of wood you use in a wood-heated stove is another consideration. Some woods are light and thus burn too quickly to produce adequate levels of heat; some produce an unpleasant odor, and others generate high levels of soot. Generally, favored woods are dense woods, weighing about 40 pounds per cubic foot, that are seasoned 6 months or more. These include white ash, yellow birch, American beech, American elm, sugar maple, Douglas fir, and several varieties of oak and pine. Though alder and cedar generate an appealing fragrance, they aren't known for their heat-producing qualities. Manufactured logs of compressed sawdust are extremely dense, with almost twice the heating value of birch.

What size wood stove? No quick formula exists for determining the correct size of a wood stove, since so many variables are involved in heating a sauna with wood: the type

of wood used for fuel, the design of the stove, the efficiency of the flue, ventilation, and any fireproof wall surfaces in the sauna that would conduct heat out of the stoveroom. Manufacturers' specifications usually can help you select the correct size wood stove.

Stove Stones

Stones are important to the sauna stove because, when hot enough, they distribute soft, pleasant heat evenly throughout the stoveroom (heat that comes directly from electrical elements tends to be harsh, strong, and uncomfortable). They maintain a proper stoveroom temperature because they can store heat well, and they are necessary for the burst of löyly (steam) that results when a dipperful of water is poured over them.

Stones considered best for sauna use are fist-size rocks such as granite that have been formed by intense exposures to heat and pressure. They store heat efficiently and—unlike sedimentary rocks which can crack, crumble, even explode under the pressure of high heat—they are unaffected by temperature extremes.

Prefabricated sauna stoves almost always come with a supply of stones, often black peridotite quarried in Finland. After about 5 years of regular use the sauna stones will "wear out," and you can purchase a new supply from sauna dealers.

In the stove, the stones should be loosely packed to allow for good air circulation, the larger ones on the bottom and smaller ones on top.

Accessories and Custom Touches

The simplest sauna usually is equipped with a thermometer, a bucket, and a long-handled ladle— you need to know the stoveroom temperature, and you need water

Sauna accessories include vihta, bucket and ladle, scrub brush, sauna hygrometer.

to pour over the hot stones if you want bursts of steam to fill the air during the bath.

More elaborate saunas may be equipped with hygrometers to measure air moisture, adjustable wooden headrests, scrub brushes, a clock, a sandglass timer, cork bench covers, an automatic humidifier, and vihtas. They may also contain (to the distress of sauna traditionalists) a telephone jack, an intercom, and an audio transducer that transmits stereo music into the sauna.

Thermometers and hygrometers.
Sauna thermometers are either bi-metallic or liquid-filled and are made of metal, ceramic, brass, chrome, or wood. They give either Fahrenheit or Celsius readings, sometimes both.

A hygrometer, an instrument that measures relative humidity, is sometimes combined with a thermometer into a "hygrotherm" or "sauna-hygro."

When you install these devices, locate them on a wall away from the stove, door, or ventilator, and about 6 inches from the ceiling, where they will give more accurate readings.

Buckets and ladles. Wood buckets are the most popular, though perhaps the least practical, choice for saunas because they suit the esthetics of the custom so well.

Metal and plastic buckets also are suitable in a sauna, but you must take care not to leave a plastic bucket too near the heat source.

The ladles you use to throw water onto sauna stones should be at least

15″ long and made of wood or metal with a wooden handle.

Vihtas. Used to stimulate blood circulation and add a pleasing scent to the sauna, vihtas are broomlike bunches of leafy twigs (traditionally birch) gathered in late spring or early summer when leaves are tender. In the sauna, bathers use vihtas to whisk themselves (and each other) lightly from head to foot.

You can buy dried vihtas from some sauna distributors; you also can easily make your own from twigs collected from broadleaf trees whose leaves have a fresh, delicate aroma: birch, maple, oak, eucalyptus, hazel, and mountain ash, among others. Using rope or twine, tie the twigs in small bunches about 20″ long, the leaves shiny side out, and hang them up to dry in a cool, dark room. Or freeze them in plastic bags (thaw at room temperature) to have a continuous supply on hand.

Before using a dried vihta, let it soak briefly in warm water, or spill water onto the sauna stones through the leaves and let the whisk absorb steam until its leaves soften. Whisks are usually good for one, no more than two, saunas.

Alternatives to the leafy vihta are soft scrub brushes you can use either in the sauna or shower, and the loofah—a coarse, cylindrical sponge that actually is the dried interior of a gourd.

Curing the Sauna

After your stoveroom is assembled or built, it's important to prepare or "cure" it before you indulge in your first heat bath. Curing a sauna is a fairly simple matter of removing construction debris and allowing the stove to burn off coatings that protect it during shipping and installation.

First, sweep down the sauna ceilings, walls, and floor to eliminate wood shavings, chips, and sawdust. Then vacuum everything, including corners and benches.

Next, using a damp cloth and bucket of warm water, wipe down the ceiling, walls, benches, light fixtures, stove, railing, and floor. Rinse off sauna rocks.

Now, prop the sauna door open and turn on the heater for about 30 minutes. (Don't worry if the stove begins to smoke—it's just burning off protective coatings.)

Last, close the sauna door, bring the room temperature to about 200°F/93°C, and leave it there for 5 or 6 hours. Now the sauna is ready for use.

Care of the Sauna

The most you usually ever need to do to a sauna is scrub it down occasionally with liquid household cleanser to remove perspiration stains and odors from the wood.

After each bath, it's also a good idea to ventilate the room so wood surfaces can dry. Prop any duckboards against the wall, and wash out the wood bucket after each use. Fill it with fresh water and let it stand so the wood doesn't dry out, split, and leak.

In wood-heated saunas it is important to keep the floor free of debris, and to regularly remove ashes from the fire box.

How to Take a Sauna

No sauna enthusiast is without his or her particular style when it comes to the bathing process, though all agree that the traditional heat bath must be approached leisurely. Allow time for the sauna to ripen, so that when you enter the stoveroom its heat will feel pleasant and inviting. Then set aside adequate time for the number of visits you like in the sauna, and for cooling off and rest periods between. Allow time, too, at the end of the bath to relax and perhaps indulge in a light snack.

How to Take a Sauna

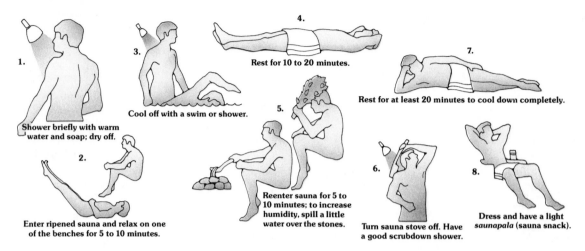

1. Shower briefly with warm water and soap; dry off.

2. Enter ripened sauna and relax on one of the benches for 5 to 10 minutes.

3. Cool off with a swim or shower.

4. Rest for 10 to 20 minutes.

5. Reenter sauna for 5 to 10 minutes; to increase humidity, spill a little water over the stones.

6. Turn sauna stove off. Have a good scrubdown shower.

7. Rest for at least 20 minutes to cool down completely.

8. Dress and have a light *saunapala* (sauna snack).

The following are only general guidelines for a heat bath; you'll soon have your own favorite pattern.

1. Adjust thermostat (electric and gas-heated rooms) to desired temperature—usually 160° to 195°F/ 71° to 91°C. For wood stoves, kindle a fire and stack dry wood nearby so you can feed the fire when necessary.

2. Remove clothing (you should take only a towel with you into the sauna), eyeglasses or contact lenses, and any jewelry or watches that can become uncomfortably hot or damaged by the sauna's heat.

3. Shower briefly with warm water and soap.

4. In the stoveroom sit or recline on a bench where the heat feels comfortable.

5. After 5 to 15 minutes, when you have begun to perspire freely, leave the sauna. (WARNING: Stay no longer than 30 minutes in the sauna; excessive exposure can be harmful.)

6. Shower again, or take a swim, or—if you're hardy—cool off with a roll in the snow. (There's no hard and fast rule that says you must shower or swim in cold water, or dive into a snowbank after a sauna, but most people who practice these rituals find the radical temperature change—sometimes as much as 200°F/93°C—invigorating.)

7. Rest for 10 to 20 minutes to allow your body to cool down further.

8. Return to the sauna. On your second visit spill small amounts of water (two or three dipperfuls at most) onto the stove stones to increase humidity in the room. (You are using far too much water if it spills through the heater onto the floor.) You may also whisk yourself lightly with a vihta to increase circulation.

9. Relax for at least 20 minutes after your final visit to the sauna. Shower with warm water and soap, then with cooler water to close the pores of your skin. Dress when you are fully cooled down.

10. Indulge in a *saunapala* (sauna snack)—something light but salty taken with plenty of liquids to make up for salts and water lost during the heat bath.

When to Sauna

As an appropriate prelude to Sunday, many Finns like to take a sauna on Saturday evening, when there's plenty of time for the ritual. Today, however, customs have adapted to accommodate people who like saunas in the morning, before work and after exercising; or in the evening after a strenuous work day, or following an afternoon of golf or skiing. Some people enjoy a brief sauna before an evening out.

Most people limit saunas to once or twice a week, although when and how frequently you like a heat bath is strictly a matter of personal preference.

A Word of Caution

Under most circumstances—particularly if you enjoy good health—the sauna generates an invigorating sense of well-being. But since it stimulates the cardiovascular system the same way jogging or tennis does, some individuals need to use more caution. You should not use the sauna if:

1) you have high blood pressure, respiratory or heart disease, serious circulatory problems, or a chronic illness such as diabetes or epilepsy, unless you first check with your physician;

2) you are taking antibiotics, tranquilizers or stimulants, or any other drugs which might be affected by speeded-up metabolism;

3) you are under the influence of alcohol or drugs—they impair judgment, and you can get a nasty burn if you lose your balance and come into contact with the hot stove. (Deaths due to dehydration have even been known to occur when individuals have passed out in the sauna.)

You also should wait at least an hour before taking a sauna if you've just eaten a large meal; and, if in the sauna you begin to feel dizzy, nauseated, or uncomfortably hot, or if your pulse is beating abnormally fast, leave the stoveroom immediately. And if you're pregnant, ask your physician about using the sauna.

Index